ALL THE Little Miracles

*A Story of Survival, Hope, and Victory
in the Face of Devastating Loss*

A Memoir

CAROL HUEBSCH REEVES

ARCHWAY
PUBLISHING

This book is a work of non-fiction. Unless otherwise noted, the author and the publisher make no explicit guarantees as to the accuracy of the information contained in this book and in some cases, names of people and places have been altered to protect their privacy.

Archway Publishing books may be ordered through booksellers or by contacting:

Archway Publishing
1663 Liberty Drive
Bloomington, IN 47403
www.archwaypublishing.com
844-669-3957

Because of the dynamic nature of the Internet, any web addresses or links contained in this book may have changed since publication and may no longer be valid. The views expressed in this work are solely those of the author and do not necessarily reflect the views of the publisher, and the publisher hereby disclaims any responsibility for them.

Any people depicted in stock imagery provided by Getty Images are models, and such images are being used for illustrative purposes only. Certain stock imagery © Getty Images.

Cover Image: (l-r) Beav, Scotty, Dann, Carol, Chip and Heather Swallow, 1972

ISBN: 978-1-6657-1610-9 (sc)
ISBN: 978-1-6657-1608-6 (hc)
ISBN: 978-1-6657-1609-3 (e)

Library of Congress Control Number: 2021924827

Print information available on the last page.

Archway Publishing rev. date: 01/25/2022

Author's Note

It has taken me forty years to tell my story—to revisit the past through the kinder, gentler lens of age. Memory can sometimes be an elusive and unreliable companion. Circumstances surrounding some events escape me completely, while others return only as fleeting and faded snapshots. But some memories play in my head like videos, vivid to the last detail.

Prologue

December 7, 1975

It was raining the morning Scotty died. Of course it was.

The phone rang at 6:00 a.m., waking me from a sound sleep. In a fog, I groped the nightstand, hunting for the receiver. It was the floor nurse at the Clinical Center of the National Institutes of Health (NIH). Scotty wasn't doing well, and Dr. Peebles wanted me there right away. My heart began to pound. *No, God, please no.*

I had watched *Cat on a Hot Tin Roof* with Liz Taylor and Burl Ives until well after midnight. Exhausted yet sleepless, I found watching someone else's tragedy a comforting distraction. Pulling on my jeans, I grabbed the phone and pushed 0 for an operator to order the courtesy van. No need to state my destination. The van served the National Institutes of Health Clinical Center exclusively.

From the sharp voice of the operator, it was clear it wasn't Martha or Geraldine, the regular morning desk clerks who knew me—who knew Scotty. Their voices would have been warm with concern. This voice sounded gruff and irritable. "It's raining; the vans are backed up," she barked.

"Then call me a cab—please. I need to be there—Doctor Peebles wants me to be there." I hung up, not waiting for an answer.

Trying to get my head together, I paused and then dialed Chip's number in Milwaukee. His wife answered. She sounded sleepy. When she heard my voice, she passed the phone without comment.

"You need to get back here."

For a change, he didn't argue. Part of me hated him for not being with his son, but the rest of me—the selfish, devastated, exhausted part—was relieved not to have to deal with him now. But Chip needed to know Scotty's condition had worsened. He said he would come.

I pulled a long red sweater over my black turtleneck. It was freezing. December rain in Washington crawled into your bones in a way Wisconsin snow never did. I was always cold. My raincoat hung behind the thick plastic pleat that passed for a closet door. *What a dump*, I thought for the thousandth time. But I couldn't complain. Reservations were hard to come by, and this room was a godsend. I was supposed to be in Milwaukee this week. It was pure luck I had a room at all.

Flipping off the light, I let myself out into the damp morning and headed down the cement stairwell and into the rain. I picked my way around a wire construction fence. My room was in the United Inn Annex, which necessitated a trip outside to the main lobby. My feet got colder as my canvas sneakers soaked up water from the broken sidewalk, where pools of mud were collecting.

My eyes swept the lobby. I longed for a familiar face or a kind smile. Patients crowded the room, no doubt heading for early chemo appointments, but they were all strangers. Even though I'd stayed at the United Inn dozens of times over the past fifteen months, not one face looked familiar.

It felt eerie, like a recurring dream from my childhood, where I come out of Gimbels department store in downtown Milwaukee. Everything outside is changed: no Wisconsin Avenue, no Milwaukee River, just blinding sunlight reflecting off the windows of tall buildings. The predictable, orderly grid of concrete streets, so carefully laid out by the city's German forbearers, has somehow morphed into a convoluted maze, and I can't find my way home.

The lobby was hot. Someone had cranked the thermostat, steaming the front windows and adding an oppressive layer to the already claustrophobic atmosphere of sickness and anxiety. All these strangers waited for the motel van, which was nowhere in sight. A cab pulled away from the door.

"Is another cab coming?" I asked the stranger at the desk. "They need me at the hospital right away."

"Wait your turn, lady," snapped a large mess of a woman who sat just inside the door, her body wedged into a gray sweat suit with a stain the size of Minnesota down her front. "We all have appointments, ya know."

A purse that looked more like an overnight bag sat on her lap. Beside her sat an emaciated girl with a bright-yellow bandana around her bald head. She pulled at the large gold hoop dangling from her ear. Her lips were a slash of red that looked almost clownish against her pale face and sunken eyes. She looked fifteen or so. On better days, she probably would have told her mother to stick it in her ear—or worse—but today, she just rolled her eyes at her mother, slumped further into the couch, and closed her eyes.

Headlights reflected off the wet pavement as a cab turned into the driveway.

"Who's next?" called the woman behind the desk. Ducking my head, I pushed out into the rain before the gray sweat suit could get out of her chair. The door whooshed closed on her angry protests. I didn't care.

As the cab pulled away from the curb, a pair of deep-set brown eyes smiled at me in the rearview mirror. It was Jim, the cabbie who drove Scotty and me from the airport last summer.

"Where's that boy of yours?" he asked. The kindness in his voice pierced my fragile shell. As my tears began to fall, his round mahogany face collapsed. "There now, Mama," he said. "There now, Mama." I opened the window and gulped cold air and rain. *No, God, not yet.*

The cab came to an abrupt halt as it approached the circular drive to the Clinical Center. Cars and vans were everywhere, honking and weaving, maneuvering for position under the steel overhang. Doctors, nurses, and orderlies poured through the revolving doors. Hospital rounds began at seven. Throwing a wad of bills over the front seat, I jumped out. It would be quicker on foot. Jim called after me, but the noise and chaos swallowed his words. I think he said he would pray for us.

The revolving door deposited me into the crowded lobby. The familiar antiseptic smell, now mixed with heat and wet wool, was stifling. A sea of people jockeyed for position in front of the elevator doors, ignoring the "walk up one flight and down two" sign. Changing course, I headed for the stairs. By the third-floor landing, my lungs were exploding. I had to stop to catch my breath and slow the racing of my heart—and my mind. *Please, not today. Help me, God.* The elevator ding broke into my thoughts. I joined the crowded car for the rest of the ride up.

The double doors of the pediatric oncology wing swung open. I could see a flurry of activity in the hall outside Scotty's room. Mary, Scotty's roommate's mom, stood with her arms full of odds and ends from her son Jack's nightstand. She looked up, and her eyes filled with tears as they met mine. I realized then what was happening. Two burly orderlies rolled Jack's bed toward the door. They were moving him to another room. Scotty's eyes, dark and sunken behind his oxygen mask, followed the bed as it moved out of sight. *He knows*, I thought.

Dropping my coat on the floor, I sat on the bed and took Scotty's hand in mine. Our eyes met as I leaned down to kiss his forehead, but we didn't speak. Somebody cranked his bed into a sitting position, the pillows propped behind him. Neither of the two nurses flanking his bed looked familiar.

It was Tuesday, Janet's day off. As his primary care nurse, she would be devastated not to be with him now. Janet had been his closest friend and confidante through the long weeks he spent in laminar airflow, the germ-free unit to which he was confined each time the toxic chemo knocked his white cells down to zero. Scotty was her first primary care patient. She was very special to all of us. The room felt empty and quiet with the other bed gone, the heavy door closing out the familiar ebb and flow of voices from the hall—the oxygen machine's soft hiss magnified in the silence. No one spoke.

The room was hot, but it occurred to me that removing my red sweater would leave me all in black, and I didn't want to be wearing all black. Could I be sitting on Scotty's bed concerned about my clothes? The sense of helplessness and inadequacy was overwhelming. I squeezed his hand and hung on.

Later, Dr. Peebles came in and stood for a while. He and Scotty acknowledged one another, but still, nobody spoke. Scotty was just too exhausted, and Dr. Peebles had run out of words.

Someone knocked. It was Scotty's fifteen-year-old friend Patti Brown asking if she could come in for a while. He brightened when he saw her and raised his hand. She did the same. I got up, hugged her, and stepped into the hall.

They were good friends and frequent companions over the long months at NIH, while each battled a different form of cancer—two teens forced into an adult world before their time. The other kids teased her about him, but she didn't mind. Shortly after Scotty died, Patti sent me a letter, including a poem she had written about him. She said she had been afraid to send it, afraid it would make me sad. But her mom and dad and the NIH nurses urged her to share it. I was glad she did. The words of her letter and poem still bring me comfort.

It looked more like evening than morning outside as rain pelted against the windows. In the hall, I caught sight of the front page of the *Washington Post* folded and left on a chair. It was December 7, Pearl Harbor Day. My namesake, Scotty's cousin Carol, had been born on December 7, fifteen years earlier. How delighted Lawrie and I were to have our babies delivered just nine months apart. *They will be lifelong friends*, we thought. But Lawrie and little Carol had moved to California, and we barely found time to talk these days.

When Patti slipped out of the room, tears rolled down her cheeks. I returned to my seat on the edge of the bed and stroked Scotty's arm. There were tears in his eyes too. His hands were turning blue. "It's all right; Momma's here," I crooned, much like when he was a little boy and had an earache. "It's all right; Momma's here." Soon his eyes closed, and he lay quietly, seeming to sleep.

We stayed there, the strange nurses and I, listening to the sound of the oxygen machine and the rain, thinking our own thoughts.

"Answer the phone." Scotty's voice startled me. It was the first he'd spoken all morning. His eyes were open, and he was looking at the nightstand where the phone lay silent. "Answer the phone," he said again, sounding more insistent this time.

"But the phone isn't ringing, sweetheart." He looked at me, confused, and then lay back and closed his eyes. "Never mind."

Those were the last words he ever said. The three of us looked at each other. Then the nurse nearest the door slipped into the hall. When she returned, Dr. Peebles was at her side. He put his hand on my shoulder and asked how I was doing. The human touch felt welcome. It was so lonely in that room.

Then Scotty's breath caught in his throat—just once. I looked up, but his eyes were still closed. He didn't seem to be choking. He looked peaceful. Without warning, Dr. Peebles removed the oxygen mask from Scotty's face and placed a rubber cone over his mouth and nose. The quiet of the morning gave way to organized chaos as Dr. Peebles and the two strange nurses began working on him. Others came in. Someone took my arm, led me firmly across the hall to the nurses' lounge, and sat beside me holding my hand. I didn't know her, but she was very kind. Time seemed suspended in the air, as though held in a bubble, going neither forward nor backward.

Later I would reflect on the flurry of those last moments and hope Scotty wasn't aware of them. At the time, my only feeling was a strange, frozen calm and a love for the men and women who were doing everything they knew how to save my son. Do not resuscitate was not an option for research patients at NIH—at least not in 1976. They were all about the business of saving lives. So there I sat in the nurses' lounge, clinging to the hand of a stranger, while they pronounced Scotty dead.

Sometime later, Dr. Peebles came in. He sat down and told me what a wonderful gift Scotty had been to all of them in the pediatric oncology program, how he seemed to understand his treatment and was proud of his part in the fight. He believed others might live because of what he had done. Then, very gently, Dr. Peebles asked if I would like to go in and see him.

Together, we crossed the hall to Scotty's room. It was eerily quiet now. The oxygen equipment had disappeared. Even the rain had paused.

Scotty wore a fresh hospital gown, and the lights were turned low. We stood together near the foot of the bed. I dropped Dr. Peebles's hand and moved toward the head of the bed, reaching out to touch Scotty's face. It was so cold. After a few minutes, Dr. Peebles asked if I would like to stay with him by myself for a while.

"No, I don't think so. He's not here anymore." As sure as I have been of anything in my life, I knew my Scotty had left that place. We turned and left the room.

One

1960

"Who gives this woman to be married to this man?" Father Stimpson looked over the wireframes of his half-glasses, waiting.

"Her mother and I." Daddy's voice was quiet but firm. Mom would be pleased with the nod to women in this modern response to the age-old question. Placing my hand in Chip's, Daddy backed carefully around the snowy mound of my wedding dress to join Mom in the front pew.

It was June 18, 1960, and all was right with the world. I was marrying my love, handsome, fun-loving Chip Swallow, and officially on my way to becoming a wife and mother—a common goal among girls coming of age in the fifties. At that moment, my BA in English literature paled in comparison to my marriage license. It was an important rite of passage.

I was too nervous to ponder the symbolism of the Great Hand-Off. In my secure world, I was simply passing from one feathered nest to another.

We were exhausted by the wedding day. Wedding plans had dominated the family landscape since we announced our engagement the previous fall. Though the youngest of three girls, I was the first to marry. Our mother made the most of it, concerned that my older sisters, Holly and Lawrie, might never make it down the aisle. They were twenty-five and twenty-eight, after all. She ruled over my wedding like a five-star general, leaving nothing to chance. Dresses, flowers, invitations, photographer, menus, music, even tastefully engraved thank-you notes had been in the works for months. Our recreation room looked like the fine china department at Marshall Fields & Company, as wedding gifts poured in.

The ceremony took place at Saint Christopher's Episcopal Church in the bucolic countryside of River Hills, Wisconsin, a stone's throw from the Milwaukee Country Club. It was there, after the service, Chip and I would greet two hundred guests at a cocktail reception "with heavy hors d'oeuvres." Having been a bridesmaid four times that year, it was a thrill and a relief to be the one wearing white.

As the sun set on that beautiful day, Chip and I danced our first dance, sipped champagne with arms entwined, stuffed cake in each other's mouths, and tossed the bouquet and garter to our bridal party. Finally, pelted by enough uncooked rice to feed a small country, we dashed offstage into the golden sunlight of our future. To me, marriage was the exciting last act of my childhood rather than the first act of the rest of my life. Other than contemplating a few names for our perfect children, I had imagined little beyond the excitement of the wedding day. What could I have been thinking?

Two

The "golden sunlight of our future" began with six weeks in Europe. Chip's older sister, Susy, lived in Rome with her husband, Walter, and their two young sons. Because they were unable to make the wedding, Chip's mother decided we should visit them. And, as long as we were going to Italy, why not visit some other countries? Consulting no one, she booked a stateroom on the USS *Independence* from New York to Naples and reserved two spaces on a European tour scheduled to gallop through nine countries in three weeks. We would leave the tour from the last stop in Cannes and fly to Rome for a weeklong stay in a *pensione* near Susy and Walter's. All told, we would be gone until early August.

Just one problem. Chip and I had planned to delay our honeymoon until fall. His mother knew this. We wanted to spend the summer on Pine Lake, a beautiful spring-fed lake west of Milwaukee, where the Swallows had a summer home. Chip was eager to race his new sailboat and I to begin nesting in the cute caretaker's cottage that was to be our summer home. And we wanted to go to the Caribbean islands.

When Chip told me his mother had given us our honeymoon for a wedding gift, the offer seemed generous and welcome. However, when I heard she had decided not only when we would go but where we would go, I balked.

"We can't say no," Chip said. "She has made all the reservations, even put down a deposit on the tour. Besides, when will we ever be able to afford a trip to Europe? Might as well take advantage of the offer." Later, when I told my parents about the gift and my disappointment, they agreed with

Chip. It might be years before such an opportunity presented itself again. How generous of Janet. Of course we should go. Wasn't I a lucky girl?

Was I a lucky girl? What nut wouldn't want to go to Europe on her honeymoon? Still, it bothered me that Chip had abandoned our plans so quickly. His inability to disagree with his mother began to make me uneasy.

At first, his concern for her seemed thoughtful. The spring before our engagement, his dad had died suddenly of a stroke at just forty-nine years old. It seemed natural that we would spend more time with his widowed mother and try not to upset her. The winter before our wedding, the three of us spent just about every Sunday driving to Pine Lake to check on the redecorating of the caretaker cottage that was to be ours. It sat across the road from the big house, laundry house, barn, tennis court, boathouse, putting green, sizeable permanent grass pier, and rolling green lawns that were the Swallow estate. It was all beautiful.

Bundled in our winter coats, we would sit in the unheated living room of the cottage, sharing a picnic lunch his mother had prepared for the occasion, often joined by her decorator. Though the redecorating was for us, I followed Chip's lead and agreed with everything his mother proposed. That wasn't too difficult. She had fabulous taste, and her decorator friend was a delightful character full of good ideas. Nonetheless, I was aware of the control she exercised over our lives. My mother-in-law terrified me. Her mercurial personality, so familiar to her family, frightened me from the start. Janet Swallow was a big-boned bully of a woman who ran the show—every show. Chip's dad, King Swallow, was a gentle soul who suffered from alcoholism and a serious stutter. I doubt the man ever finished a sentence after marrying Janet. Before his death, King always treated me with kindness and respect, no doubt to counter his wife's erratic behavior. Chip and his sister, Susy, had tiptoed around the edges of their mother's rages all their lives. Though at times she was friendly, even fun, the good times harbored a nagging fear of what roiled beneath the surface. Today, she might be diagnosed as bipolar and medicated accordingly. Instead, her personality disorder raged on, untreated, throughout her lifetime.

Rocking the boat was not my style, so when she took over our honeymoon, I thanked her profusely and applied for a passport. By the time we returned to Milwaukee in August, I was pregnant.

Three

The whoosh of the heavy door swinging open played right into my crazy dream, but the sudden glare from the ceiling light brought me awake. It was my fifth and final night in the maternity ward of Columbia Hospital, a typical stay for a new mother in 1961. A nurse was heading toward my bed with a bundle tucked into the crook of her arm. It was Scotty, and he was hungry. The big, round clock on the wall read 3:30 a.m.

"He's a big one," the nurse said, looking down at Scotty. "Slept four hours straight without a peep. We don't see that often."

Scotty had been born on March 21, 1961. His legal name was Kingston Francis Swallow III, after his dad and grandfather, but Chip and I had agreed ahead of time if he were to carry the cumbersome family name, we would call him "Scotty."

His ten pounds, four ounces weight was a constant source of conversation in the nursery. To me, he looked tiny, and four hours of sleep didn't feel like nearly enough. My friend Marion dubbed Columbia Hospital the Hotel Paymore. Five days in a private room could cost as much as $700. Health insurance was a thing of the future. We thought the price scandalous, but it was like a vacation in many ways—no cooking or cleaning, and the night nurses gave great back rubs.

I struggled with the cumbersome nursing bra and then reached eagerly for my baby. Nursing was one of the few privileges allowed a new mother in the maternity ward. Babies stayed in the nursery like little chicks in rows of transparent plastic cribs. They were allowed out only at mealtime. If one wanted to peek between meals, it required a painful hike down the hall, a tap on the nursery glass, and pointing and gesturing in hopes a nurse would bring your baby to the window.

One of the first nights, while Scotty and I were wrestling with the elusive art of breastfeeding, little motorboat sounds came from his swaddled receiving blanket. Realizing a dirty diaper would not enhance the feeding experience, I quickly undid the diaper pins and held them in my teeth while folding the soiled diaper and wiping his little bottom with Kleenex from the nightstand. Then I fashioned a new diaper from his burp cloth and anchored it in place. When the nurse came for him, I told her what had occurred. While I was not expecting a blue ribbon, her scolding was a surprise. She informed me in no uncertain terms that babies are carefully weighed in and out of the nursery (diapers and poop included), and a rogue diaper change could result in a false reading. It seemed in 1961, women didn't become mothers at the hour of birth, but five days later when they went home with their babies.

As Scotty latched onto my sore nipple, I looked down in wonder at his precious face, his little fists with their pin-drop nails clenched against the blue veins of my breast. He was perfect, his pink shell ears lying flat against his head and tiny, wispy eyelashes. The blond peach fuzz covering his head was so fine he looked bald. It was hard to reconcile this angel with the demon stomping my bladder and kicking my ribs for months. A dizzying wave of love and well-being swept over me. I would love this precious baby with all my heart for the rest of my life. No one would ever hurt him. Not on my watch. Not ever. Tomorrow, the three of us would go home and begin life as a family. Now I was the luckiest girl in the world.

At 9:00 a.m. the following day, Mom peeked around the partially closed door of my hospital room. It surprised me. The staff was strict about visiting hours on the maternity floor, and besides, we'd be home in a few hours. She hurried over and kissed the top of my head.

"Hi, darling. Did you and Scotty have a good night?"

"He slept four hours straight. Everyone was pretty excited. What are you doing here?"

Mom didn't answer right away but took my hand in hers. A chill went up my spine.

"Did something happen to Daddy?"

"Your father is fine. Everyone is fine. But I need to tell you something, and I want you to stay calm." If Mom was warning me to stay calm, I probably couldn't.

"What happened?"

It seems Chip had called them at 2:00 a.m. from the police station, charged with drunken driving and leaving the scene of an accident. He needed bail and a ride home. Even in his impaired state, he was smart enough to call my parents rather than his mother. She would have killed him. Daddy told him to sleep it off. He would pick him up in the morning. Aside from being angry, my father knew it would take time to round up bail money on a Sunday morning.

"Was anyone hurt?" I asked, trying to process the enormity of Mom's words.

No one was injured. An elderly couple was stopped at a traffic light when Chip rammed into the back of their car and then backed up and drove around them without stopping. The police had little trouble following the line of fluid leaking from his radiator. Daddy had bailed him out an hour ago and taken him to the Athletic Club for a steam bath.

While most of the emotions my hormone-battered body felt that morning are unclear, I do know all the sunshine went out of our homecoming. To say the news was shocking wouldn't be quite honest. Chip's drinking had become a bone of contention over the nine months of our marriage. He loved a party. I knew that when we married. But then so did lots of guys. We were young and carefree, kids just out of college, responsible for no one but ourselves. Alcoholism was an adult problem, and we didn't think of ourselves as adults. At least not yet. Chip grew up with an alcoholic father who broke promises and missed important events in his life. He often said he would never do that to his kids, and

I believed him. Neither of us realized the chances were greater than average that he would do just that.

When Chip arrived at the hospital at noon, he was so hungover that talking was difficult. Despite his visit to the steam room, the sour smell of alcohol lingered. Our ride home was quiet. I sat in the passenger seat, Scotty held tightly in my arms. Seat belts were still a thing of the future. Chip felt ill, and I obsessed with anger, self-pity, and the enormous challenge of taking care of our first baby.

Mom's car was in the driveway when we got home. She had brought over the bassinet we had all slept in as babies, wholly redone in soft yellow cotton with a dotted Swiss overlay. The large wicker wash basket lined with tufted cotton batting was not something that would get today's Consumer Product Safety Commission seal of approval. Still, to me, it was gorgeous, and I was touched.

Standing in the doorway was the baby nurse that Mother Swallow had hired to "help us through" the first week. She looked like she was a hundred years old, but her references had been good, and evidently, we were lucky she could fit us into her busy schedule. When first suggested, the idea of a baby nurse seemed silly. Surely we could handle one baby. But at that moment, seeing her there was a relief.

When Mom left, and Scotty had nursed, we all lay down for a nap. I'm not sure who needed it more. We woke to a soft knock on the bedroom door. The nurse wondered if we wanted our dinner on trays. Lord, I'd forgotten the special welcome home dinner I'd arranged with all of Chip's favorite foods. It was a suggestion from my natural childbirth class. The idea was to make the new father feel loved and appreciated. I almost choked on the irony.

Chip somehow managed to get the trays upstairs, but once the door was closed, it was clear he wasn't going to eat a bite. It was unthinkable to send the steak and baked potato back untouched, so, wrapped in a diaper, what remained of the special dinner went out onto the window ledge. Tomorrow there would be time to sneak the package into the garbage.

Chip got the trays back to the kitchen before falling asleep again, this time for the night. Angry and exhausted, my stitches killing me, I headed for the nursery to watch our new baby sleep.

Chip's accident and subsequent DUI (driving under the influence) made the front page of the *Milwaukee Sentinel* Monday morning under a scathing headline.

Mother Swallow was livid—not because Chip had been drunk and hit another car, but because he had called my parents instead of her. She at least could have phoned the publisher of the paper and had the story buried. Chip, on the other hand, was contrite and apologetic. When the court imposed a fine and revoked his driver's license for a year, he thought it well-deserved and didn't complain. We both thought he had learned his lesson.

Four

We wanted a family, so neither of us was dismayed to learn I was pregnant. My idea of a perfect family was two boys two years apart, followed in three years by two girls two years apart. Imagine my delight when our second son, Stephen Joseph, was born on Scotty's second birthday. We were right on track. To our surprise, however, twenty months later, Dann Haynes arrived.

Looking back on the 1960s always reminds me of a convention I attended in 1989. The big social event of the convention was a costume party with a Sixties theme. The Shirelles, an aging female quartet from that era, entertained with songs to which most of us knew all the words. Haight Ashbury and Woodstock-inspired beatnik costumes filled the ballroom. Most men wore longhaired wigs, headbands, and beads. The women, barefooted in flowing skirts and peasant blouses, had flowers woven in their hair. My costume took far less imagination. With a large pillow from the hotel stuffed under a loose-fitting top, I went as a pregnant woman. Our babies were born in 1961, 1963, 1964, and 1968. My 1960s were a blur of morning sickness, diapers, bottles, and unrelenting exhaustion. The time not spent feeding, bathing, or playing referee was spent cleaning, washing, ironing, shopping, and cooking meals. The learning curve was steep.

Growing up as the youngest of three offered little opportunity for experience with little ones other than a few hapless stabs at babysitting. There I learned that infants could not tell you why they are fussing or crying. I had no idea how to make them stop, which left me a little afraid of babies.

At first, we spent summers in our caretaker's cottage at Pine Lake. We rented homes in town in the winter, mostly from older couples seeking someone to watch over their houses while they wintered in Florida. It gave us a nice place to stay, and they had someone to water their plants and check their property. It was a fair trade. But moving two toddlers and a dog into someone else's home proved more than a little challenging. A puppy had joined our family the first Christmas. That poor dog. She was pushed further down the food chain with each new baby and subject to ever-increasing doses of toddler love.

We would arrive at our new winter rental late on Labor Day, following a full day of sailboat races, picnics, and packing at the lake. Then would come a mad rush through the rental house, putting everything that looked breakable or edible in a hiding spot out of the reach of little hands. Naturally, come Memorial Day, when it was time to leave, I could not remember what I hid, where I hid it, and where in the world it belonged.

The boys were good friends and great playmates. It was during those years that Scotty gave Stephen a nickname. When his prominent front teeth first came in, Scotty began calling his brother "Stever the Beaver." Before long, the whole family was calling him "Beaver." Though in later years, a shortened version of the nickname stuck. Stephen Joseph will always be Beav to family and the friends of his youth.

One year, it was well into the hot summer before our winter landlord found a pound of butter melted in his antique grandfather clock. In those days, houses had milk chutes. One marked one's order on a milk card, and the milkman filled the order early the next morning without having to come indoors. Scotty had learned to unlatch the inside milk chute door and decided to put the butter "away" for Mommy.

When our third baby was on the way, it seemed time to get a place of our own. That was easier said than done. By Labor Day of 1964, we settled for a house on the east side of Milwaukee—an okay place, but not one we loved. On November 25 of that year, Dann Haynes joined the family, and life was busier than ever. Danny's birth blessed us with three little boys under four years old. Loving and caring for them, keeping them warm, fed, clothed, and safe, was all-encompassing.

We were also fast outgrowing our little caretaker's cottage at Pine Lake, so Mother Swallow gave Chip the boathouse, a lovely two-bedroom two-bath house built over the boat slip. Over the winter, they added two more bedrooms, a third bath, a large family room, and a laundry room. I stayed in town battling morning sickness and caring for our two boys. Again Mother Swallow oversaw the decorating, and again there was no cause for complaint. The new boathouse was beautiful. Sitting right at the water's edge, it had a massive permanent grass pier jutting into Pine Lake.

We weren't the only ones having children. It seemed someone in our crowd was always pregnant—sharing maternity clothes, Johnny Jump Ups, and high chairs. Along the way, someone discovered the unwed mother programs at Catholic and Lutheran Social Services. For twelve dollars a month, plus room and board, an unwed mother would live in your home and help with child care and light housekeeping. The program was a godsend for mothers, both wed and unwed. Of course, each stay was only five or six months long, at which time we had the responsibility of taking the girls to the hospital and supporting them through labor and delivery. Over the next decade, I served as a substitute father to twelve unwed mothers. After delivery, the social services arranged for the babies to be adopted, and the women returned to their homes, most often in rural Wisconsin. Then pregnancy before marriage was considered shameful, for the girl and her family—my, how things have changed.

Help at home created time for me to begin what would become a lifetime of volunteer work. However, my motivation in those days was probably less altruistic than a pressing need to interact occasionally with people over three feet tall. The Junior League offered a fertile training ground for identifying and meeting community needs and preparing young women to be leaders in those efforts.

Five

I turned thirty in 1967. I was like most thirty-year-olds; the idea both horrified and amazed me. How did it happen so fast? Age zero to ten seemed to last forever, filled with the busy business of childhood. Eleven to twenty passed more quickly, consumed by the fun—and angst—of coming-of-age, discovering boys, and getting educated. My twenties tipped me smack into adulthood, ready or not. Days were chock full, morning to night, leaving little time for reflection or analyses.

But turning thirty gave me pause—not to search a magnifying mirror for creases and sags, but to reflect on my life. There were so many blessings. Chip and I had three healthy sons, who brought us great joy, and we were expecting our fourth child in two months. Chip's mother had remarried—a lovely man from Detroit named Dick Haynes. Dick, a lifelong bachelor, relished having a family and became a loving grandpa for our children.

We also found our dream home that year. It was in Shorewood, a suburb along the bluff of Lake Michigan, just north of Milwaukee. North Prospect Avenue was a beautiful tree-lined street in a neighborhood bursting with children of all ages. It was there that our precious Heather Ellen was born in the chilly winter of 1968. Chip's drinking was the only cloud on the horizon. Our fights were almost always caused or escalated by alcohol. Raising three active boys was physically and mentally exhausting. Like most stay-at-home moms, by the end of the day, I was as eager for Daddy's homecoming as were the kids. When he did not come home, my temperament and patience stretched pretty thin. We worked best when parenting together. Chip was a wonderful dad. He loved his kids, and they loved him. But he became a different person when he drank—one I did not like very much and one I didn't know how to deal with. The fun guy who was everybody's friend could be an abusive and sarcastic drunk. As most of our old friends were settling down to raise their families, Chip expanded his circle to include drinking buddies. There always seemed to be someone who wanted to stop for a drink after work. When would he settle down?

Six

"Pack a picnic. We are going for a ride," Chip announced as he came into the kitchen one Saturday morning in early April 1970. It sounded more like an order than a request. I concentrated on pouring more orange juice for Heather, who sat on her booster seat at the kitchen table. Chip and I hadn't spoken since last night when he rolled into bed sometime after midnight.

"I'm going to the MAC. I'll be back by eleven. I have a surprise for the kids."

With that, he patted Heather's golden curls and headed for the garage. The MAC was the Milwaukee Athletic Club. It was where Chip exercised, played squash, and hung out. This morning, I was pretty sure he would head for the steam room. Heather sat mashing milk and cheerios into a sodden mess in her bowl.

"Daddy probably bought another building." I sighed, wiping her face. "Would you like to go on a picnic to see Daddy's building?" My tone was light, attempting to mask the resentment I felt at having my day ruined.

It was one of those warm teaser days in early April when the smell of earth and sunshine hold false promise for winter-weary Milwaukeeans starved for a sign of spring. Excited voices drifted through the open window. Kids, happy to be outdoors, were taunting, cheering, laughing, and bickering, a symphony of childhood I can summon to this day. For the first time in months, the neighborhood kids spilled into the street for a pickup game of baseball.

"You can play in the den while Mommy gets us ready," I said.

Heather ran to the den window, entranced by the action in the street. "Scotty," she squealed, pointing at her big brother chasing a ball up the driveway. "Hi, Scotty."

Scotty couldn't hear her, but he saw her in the window and waved. In a neighborhood full of boys, little Heather was still considered special. Her brothers were proud of her. She often was included in their games—dubbed Penelope Pitstop after a popular TV cartoon character. But today, street baseball took precedence, and it was no place for a two-year-old. Always good-natured, Heather was content to watch from the window. I sighed and headed back to the kitchen. Thirty minutes ago, the day had stretched before me like a gift of peace not often enjoyed by the mother of nine-, seven-, and six-year-old boys.

At eleven o'clock, I yodeled, and the kids clamored in the back door, rosy-cheeked and breathless from the exercise. Some mothers hollered to summon their children from play, some whistled, some rang a bell, but I yodeled. It was not a Swiss Alps yodel but one distinctive and loud enough to bring them running. It was a yodel I learned from my mother, who learned it from her mother.

"Where's Dad?" said Scotty, throwing himself into a chair at the kitchen table. "I'm hungry."

"He'll be here. Go wash the mud off your hands and faces, so you're ready."

By the time Chip finally pulled into the driveway, it was twelve thirty, and the kids were hungry and irritated, bickering among themselves. Chip operates by a different clock than the rest of the world. One might think by now I would be used to it, but I wasn't. To me, it was inconsiderate, another of the many points of contention growing between us.

Scotty and Beav grabbed the picnic basket and piled into the back of the station wagon with Danny. Heather sat between us on the bench-like front seat, her little plastic car seat hooked over the back. As we backed out of the driveway, I passed a box of pretzels around to keep everyone happy and then settled into my seat, determined to punish Chip for his thoughtlessness with a wall of silence. He whistled to himself, obviously pleased with his surprise and oblivious to my mood. When the boys asked where we were going, he just smiled and said, "You'll see."

By the time the car slowed, we were well into the lake country west of Milwaukee. Despite myself, I, too, was curious to know where we were going. The two-lane blacktop road wound through the country-side without a house in sight—or a person for that matter. Finally, in the middle of nowhere, Chip pulled sharply off the road onto a gravel driveway, half-hidden in a tangle of brush. "We're here!" he announced and killed the engine.

"Where?" the boys chorused, spilling out of the car.

"At Mary Hill."

I'd heard of Mary Hill. It was Marquette University's off-campus ski hill.

"What's Mary Hill?" Beav asked, looking past the flat gravel parking lot toward a gradual slope.

"It's a ski hill," said Chip. "Marquette University owned it, but it's been closed for five years. It's ours now."

"It is?" The boys were looking at Chip wide-eyed, not sure if he was serious. A feeling in the pit of my stomach told me he was.

"Yup. Mr. Buechel and I bought it from the university. We're going to start a ski club." That got their attention. "No way!" they chorused. "Like Heiliger Huegel?"

Heiliger Huegel was the private ski club to which we belonged. It had a gentle hill with a rope tow and several runs. It was a wonderful place to teach kids to ski and a much sought-after membership for Milwaukee's skiing families. I knew Heiliger Huegel had a long waiting list.

"We hope to make it better than Heiliger Huegel," Chip said. "It's going to be the best darn ski club in Wisconsin. Go on, have a look around."

"Wait!" I called. "I thought you guys were hungry."

But nobody heard. The boys were already racing toward the hill, with Heather hurrying along behind.

I whirled around and looked at Chip, dumbfounded. It wasn't just that he had bought a ski hill without discussing it—though there was some of that. A bigger worry was the rate at which he had begun to make significant investments of time and money in commercial real estate with no real education or experience.

"Come on, Carol, cheer up," he said. "You know Heiliger Huegel has a waiting list. The Milwaukee market needs another ski club, and this is going to be it. John has been looking for a career change, and he has agreed to serve as the club manager and part-owner. It was too good to pass up." With that, he opened the cooler in the back of the car, cracked a beer, and, holding it aloft, gave a toast.

"Here's to Milwaukee's newest and best ski club!"

Seven

Despite my initial reservations, the ski hill turned out to be an excellent family activity and the center of our cold-weather lives. One night, while having a drink at the Pabst Brewery Rathskeller, John and Chip debated a name for the new club. Both had heard and liked the name "Buena Vista." But this was Milwaukee. They asked the German bartender how he would say "Buena Vista" in German.

"Ausblick," he replied.

"That's it!" they agreed. And so Ausblick Ski Club was born.

All of us put our whole hearts into making Ausblick the newest and best ski club in Wisconsin. While crews spent the fall grooming the hill, an artist created a logo, and the hunt for members began. The old lodge underwent significant improvements. Large picture windows were installed, looking out onto the slopes. The centerpiece of the spacious main room was a massive circular stone fireplace, surrounded by a stone ledge wide enough to warm your boots, your bottom, or both. Members would toast many hot dogs and marshmallows over that fire. Contractors brought the kitchen up to date so members could refrigerate, heat, and prepare family picnics. A small office and locked owner's closet completed the space. How grateful we were for that closet. It saved lugging five (and eventually six) sets of skis, boots, and poles back and forth each time we went to the hill. And that was often. In season, Ausblick was open Wednesday and Friday nights, plus all day Saturdays and Sundays.

The hill was also upgraded in major ways, including the first triple-chair lift in Wisconsin and a rope tow for the beginner slope.

State-of-the-art lights were installed to accommodate night skiing. A young handyman named Dennis Evinrude was hired to help out. He was a godsend.

Those early years at Ausblick were some of our happiest. The children loved the hill, so it was a rare weekend we weren't there as a family. Chip was at his best in the great outdoors. He was a beautiful, strong skier who loved helping people, a perfect combination. He and John dedicated themselves to their ski patrol responsibilities. In the beginning, as the only ski patrollers, they were always on duty. However, soon others passed the test and took up the slack. Yet, in the early years, Ausblick was rarely open without one or both owners present.

Eight

Skiing was not something my family had done in my youth. We ice-skated, tobogganed, sledded, and bowled in the winter but never skied. Not that there weren't opportunities. My senior year in high school, a group of us signed up for the Ski Club's annual trip to Ladysmith, Wisconsin. I still remember my plot to transport contraband from Daddy's liquor cabinet in a repurposed shampoo bottle. In the end, a sleet storm ruined the skiing, and the shampoo ruined the scotch.

Then there was the experience during Christmas break from college one year. A Marquette law student who had piqued my interest the previous summer invited me for a day of skiing at Little Switzerland, a public ski hill north of Milwaukee. I was thrilled. No matter that I knew little about skiing. How hard could it be? Spending a whole day with this gorgeous boy was a dream come true. After I had borrowed baggy ski pants from my sister and rental skis and boots from the Little Switzerland ski shop, off we went.

Somehow I had failed to make clear the depth of my inexperience. The gap in our skill levels was quick to send us our separate ways. That proved a blessing. So much for spending the day together. Crawling into bed that night, exhausted, aching, and caked in Bengay, I thanked the good Lord for bringing me home in one piece. Skiing would not be part of my future.

And it wasn't. That is until our Danny was born. It was November 25, the day before Thanksgiving 1964, and I had just settled into my hospital room, flush with the thrill of producing another healthy baby when Chip came in. We had decided if it were another boy, we would name him Daniel Haynes Swallow—"Haynes" for the children's beloved Grandpa Dick, and "Daniel" because I loved the name "Danny." As it turned out, the next day, Chip's mother told us that a woman named Frances Dann married his great-grandfather George C. Swallow in 1866. We happily changed the Daniel to Dann, which seemed far more interesting. As Chip headed for the door that afternoon, he turned to me with a grin and said, "Now that we have three boys, you will have to learn to ski. No more excuses."

Three months later, I found myself standing ten thousand feet above sea level on the side of a mountain in Vail, Colorado, staring down at a dollhouse-size village. No more rented equipment for me. My skis, poles, and boots were brand new, as were my fashionable ski clothes. I couldn't wiggle my toes or feel my nose. A four-person gondola had deposited a ski instructor, two terrified beginners, and me at "Mid-Vail," where the torture would begin.

Vail was a brand-new ski area. The one-street town laid out by Milwaukee architect Fitzhugh Scott had a Bavarian vibe. Fitzhugh Scott had also built some beautiful vacation homes on the slopes above the village, including one for his niece and our good friend Barbie Hodgson and her husband, Jack. That year, when the Hodgsons invited us to join them along with some friends from Toronto for ten days in Vail, how could I say no?

A vacation this was not. Chip and the others spent their days skiing, lunching at the Red Lion, and drinking hot buttered rums. I spent my days snowplowing down the beginner hill, blessed by a thirty-minute lunch break at the Mid-Vail cafeteria. At day's end, while the others zigzagged down the mountain through the pines to our doorstep, I lugged my skis uphill from the village, blisters raw and bleeding in my boots. Was there improvement? You bet. Before we went home, I added the "stem christie" turn to my repertoire. But that was about as far as this cowardly lion would go. For years, instructors would tell me to lean downhill—out over my skis. But survival instincts told me to stay as close to the mountain as possible.

So during my time at Ausblick, and on the three or four trips we took to Vail over the coming years, my skills were never on a level with the good guys—not even with my boys, for that matter. Afraid of nothing, they were quickly outskiing me. But I did learn to love the skiing life—the fresh air, the beautiful vistas, the fun people, the open fires, and everything après ski.

Nine

I lay in bed staring at the ceiling while a snowplow worked its way up Prospect Avenue, scraping and banging over the hard-packed snow. It was a welcome diversion. The eerie silence of the neighborhood, trapped under a foot of snow, was getting on my nerves. It was 2:00 a.m., and we were well into the giant deep freeze that is winter in Wisconsin.

Chip had called hours ago to say he was on his way home, and I lay watching for the kaleidoscope of lights that crossed the ceiling when his car turned in the driveway. He had sounded so good on the phone; the meeting had been unexpected … He was sorry he hadn't called sooner … Were the kids loving the snow? Though the words were different, the music was the same. Once again, I failed to pick up on the familiar melody. By now, for sure, he was either drunk or dead. Did it really matter which? Tomorrow would bring the usual rehash—he as contrite as his pounding head would allow, and I, wearing my martyrdom of exhaustion like a crown of thorns, beating him over the head with my pain. It was a familiar cycle—one I seemed powerless to break. My body was beyond exhaustion, but my churning brain jumped from one chilling image to another. What if he lay unconscious in the snow somewhere? *Damn him!*

It felt like hours before the spray of lights swept across the ceiling. But the car stopped at the front door instead of pulling around to the garage. A door slammed. Staying back in the shadows, I went to the bedroom window, which looked down on the front door, and nudged the curtain aside. A man was making his way around the hood of the car toward the passenger door, his breath coming in frozen puffs. I didn't recognize the man or the car. As he helped the passenger from the front seat, I saw Chip's camel's hair coat and Tyrolean hat. He was unsteady on his feet. The stranger was helping him through the snow toward the door. I grabbed my bathrobe and flew down the stairs. The jerk was leaning on the bell.

"Shush," I hissed, opening the door. "You'll wake the kids."

The man helped Chip into the front hall.

"You must be Carol. Old Chipper here seems to have had a few too many. His car is at the parking garage at Broadway and Jackson. Figured he could pick it up tomorrow."

"Thanks so much." My voice sounded polite, as if the man were dropping off a load of dry cleaning instead of my husband. Chip stood swaying, a stupid grin on his round face. His eyes, narrow on their best days, were mere slits. Stumbling forward, he threw his arm across my shoulders, almost sending us both to our knees. My stomach lurched at the stench of alcohol and cigarettes.

"Have you met the perfect Miss Carol?" he crooned in a singsongy voice, his lips curved upward in a smile that didn't reach his eyes.

"Just had the pleasure, pal. Gotta run." The man patted Chip on the back and headed for the door.

"You all right?" he mouthed with his back to Chip.

"Just fine. Thanks again for bringing him home." That polite little voice again.

Was I sure I would be all right? Chip was a mean drunk. But it was mortifying to stand so exposed in front of this stranger. As his car backed out of the driveway, I switched off the porch light and spun around to face my husband. All the angst and anger that had built over the last few hours dissolved in a wave of disgust. Exhausted and determined to avoid a fight, I headed back upstairs.

Ten

One day in early fall, while I was making lunch for the kids, the doorbell rang. The stranger at the door asked if this were the Swallow residence. When I nodded, he handed over an official-looking envelope addressed to Chip and a clipboard for my signature on the line next to Chip's name.

"Thank you," I called as he headed down the driveway.

Tossing the envelope on the chest in the foyer, I returned to the kitchen. When the boys headed back to school, it was time for Heather's nap—the envelope was forgotten.

The following morning, Chip was ripping it open as he came into the kitchen. He swore under his breath as he scanned the contents. I thought it probably had to do with one of his apartment buildings.

"Is anything wrong?" I asked.

He said he could handle it.

Three days later, another man appeared with another letter and soon after, a third. By then, I knew the men were process servers, and the letters were summonses for Chip to appear in court. Aside from the muttered oath that first morning, he seemed unaffected. Just a mix-up with apartment rents, he said. The letters kept coming. One night, I asked if he was going to tell me what was going on.

"You might as well know," he said. "I've got some financial problems. Not to worry. I have a lawyer on it. We're meeting Saturday morning. Come along if you can."

At 9:00 a.m. the following Saturday, we were seated in his lawyer's conference room. It was an elegant room, smelling of furniture polish, old leather, and big deals.

Chip lit a cigarette, his eyes darting around the room, lingering on everything except me. He was no stranger to spaces like this. He thrived on wheeling and dealing, buying and selling, playing in the Big Time. We were silent. What was there to say after all? I'd asked what was going on and was about to find out.

The lawyer entered, carrying a bulging legal-sized folder. It was Saturday, and the office was empty. After Chip introduced me, the lawyer settled into a chair at the head of the table. The room was too quiet. I wanted to bolt. The lawyer flipped open the file and looked at us over half glasses. He took a deep breath and began reciting from notes on a yellow legal pad—a litany of lawsuits, broken contracts, deals gone sour, and mounting debt. Chip lit a fresh cigarette off the butt of the old one and blew a perfect smoke ring toward the ceiling.

"The bottom line—debts exceed assets by hundreds of thousands of dollars, and you are being sued for commingling funds." He dropped the legal pad back on the table and concentrated on cleaning his lenses. I took a deep breath and looked at the wall above Chip's head, unable to look at him. The silk cocoon that had surrounded me since childhood was evaporating into the rarified air of this elegant conference room, and I was helpless to stop it. As unprepared as I was for this news, I didn't for a minute doubt it was true.

"There might be a chance to straighten this out and avoid bankruptcy, but I can't do it when I can't find you. You will need to come here every day: no long lunches, no more big deals. I want to be able to reach you when I need to. This battle won't be easy. We have a lot to do." Chip crushed his cigarette in the ashtray and tapped his lighter on the table, mulling over the proposition. "I can do that," he said.

"I'll get a job!" Even I was startled by my voice. I had said aloud what had been running through my head.

Chip looked up. "I don't think so, Carol." His tone was sarcastic. "We're talking real money here. What could you do?"

His words infuriated me. "I don't know, but I'll find something.

This family is my family too. I am a college graduate and a professional volunteer."

My two-year term as president of the Junior League of Milwaukee, a demanding and prestigious position, had just ended. I was sure I could find a job somewhere.

Eleven

We rode home from the lawyer's office in silence, each wrapped in our thoughts. The outcome shouldn't have surprised me, but it did. Of all the grim scenarios my fertile imagination had fashioned over the past few months, going broke wasn't one of them. The financial security that passed so seamlessly from Daddy to Chip on our wedding day seemed, if anything, more sound. Despite the Swallow wealth, we didn't live lavishly. Chip provided me with a monthly allowance, and I paid the household bills, taking great pride in maintaining meticulous records. On the rare occasion when I needed more, I had only to ask. None of the wives in our group had jobs outside the home. Our husbands were starting their careers, so we all sought ways to stretch a dollar. "One Hundred Ways to Serve Hamburger" and "Make It Now; Bake It Later" were required reading for my sewing club. Some added *The I Hate To Cook Book* to the mix. I still remember rule #1. "When in doubt, throw it out."

While other husbands were building solid careers as doctors, lawyers, bankers, and stockbrokers, Chip hopped from one venture to another. First, he sold residential real estate, then commercial; next, he became a residential real estate appraiser, then a commercial real estate appraiser. By the end of the 1960s, he was becoming a significant investor in commercial real estate. As our family grew, so did the size and scope of his investment portfolio. If I worried about anything besides the children during those years, it was Chip's drinking. It was too much and too often.

The more Chip drank, the more our personal life spiraled out of control, and the faster I ran on my little wheel of pain and confusion. Chip's drinking seemed my cross to bear—a reflection of my failure to provide the kind of atmosphere he wanted to return to at the end of his day. I know now that, in my victimhood, I was the stereotypical enabler—a poisonous yet typical cycle of doom for loved ones of alcoholics. To the world, we were a happy couple with a great life. We had four beautiful children and two beautiful homes. We raced sailboats in the summer and skied at our private ski club in the winter. The busier my life, the less time I had to deal with the reality of our shattering fairytale.

Long, wet business lunches held no stigma in the seventies, further legitimized by their IRS designation as business expenses. Many a deal was born of creativity fueled by alcohol. Chip loved the infamous three-martini lunch, which provided an all-too-safe harbor for drinkers. It worried me constantly that alcohol might cloud his judgment. But losing everything? Could it have come to that? If we just buckled down, pulled in our horns, and took hold of things, we would be fine. By the time our car turned onto Prospect Avenue, my initial shock and anger had turned to determination. The spot we were in would have frightened me had I ever gone to bed hungry or cold or alone—but I hadn't. Our current situation was a problem to be solved. Years of leadership in volunteer organizations had given me the confidence that I could make a difference. I could and would find a job. Monday morning couldn't come soon enough.

Twelve

Monday dawned cold and clear. As soon as the kids were off to school, the job search began. I settled at the large mahogany desk on the landing with a steaming cup of coffee. French doors with a Juliet balcony bathed the area in sunlight. Filled with determination, and Sunday's classified ads spread on the smooth surface before me, I began my search. It didn't take long to realize any job worth considering required training in specific fields, or at least some practical experience. No one was advertising for an aging English literature major or a dedicated volunteer. My best chance would have to come through contacts—people I knew socially or had worked with on community and nonprofit boards over the years. Today, they call that networking.

By the end of the week, it seemed everyone in Milwaukee knew Carol Swallow, ex-president of the Junior League, was looking for paid employment. There was no pretending I was looking for work for anything but financial need. Despite the women's liberation movement, most who could afford to stay home with their children still preferred to do so. While my close friends remained wonderfully supportive, I suspect others took delight in seeing the mighty fall.

Mother Swallow was horrified by my decision to get a job. She told her friends her daughter-in-law was overreacting, embarrassing the family. That didn't surprise me. Chip told his mother as little as possible about his business, and I certainly wasn't about to confide in her. As helpful as it would have been to include her powerful circle of friends on my contact list, that wasn't going to happen.

After three weeks and dozens of leads, I was no closer to gainful employment than on the first day. Many of those contacted were generous with advice, and most were generous with their time, but no one had an opening or even a solid recommendation. Guess this wasn't going to be so easy after all.

It seemed my BA in English literature, while opening the windows of my mind, had left me ill-prepared to put food on the table. In retrospect, the skills that anchored my successful future in communications did reflect the very core of a good liberal arts education. Vocabulary, writing, problem solving, decision making, and knowledge of history and the arts were all key to the creative process that is communications. But back then, I was simply trying to survive and find a job that would feed us and keep a roof over our heads.

Just as my confidence was flagging, a call came from Isabel Lillie, president of the River Edge Nature Center Board. The Junior League had helped the Whitefish Bay Women's Club fund River Edge in its early years. I still served on its board of directors. It seemed Isabel's dear friend Lois Rice, development director at Alverno College, had told her of a job opening at the Catholic college.

"When I heard Alverno was looking for a coordinator of continuing education," she said, "I thought of you immediately. You are perfect for this job. I told Lois as much."

Was she kidding? Where was Alverno College, and what was a coordinator of continuing education? It didn't sound like something for which I was qualified in any way. Grateful for her kindness, however, I agreed to call Lois that evening. What on earth did I know about college admissions?

When I finished the dishes, it was time to call the phone number Isabel had given me, but my finger froze on the dial. Why had I agreed to call a perfect stranger about a job for which I had no qualifications? Holding my breath, I dialed. It seems Lois indeed expected my call and was eager to set up an interview. Could we meet in the morning? I agreed and took down detailed driving directions. Alverno College was on the south side of the city, at least thirty minutes from my house. Despite living in Milwaukee all my life, that part of town was new to me.

Our interview the following day lasted more than two hours. Lois was a tall, striking woman with beautiful silver-blue eyes and salt-and-pepper hair. She was director of admissions at a time of rapid expansion at Alverno. The student body consisted mainly of students from the predominantly Polish south-side neighborhood that surrounded the college. Led by President Sister Joel Read, the faculty developed an exciting new liberal arts teaching model called competence-based learning (CBL). I would be the coordinator of continuing education. The new position would include holding entrance interviews with adult students, plus expanding and promoting a program of noncredit courses to attract adult women to the campus. Surprising as it may seem, continuing education was a new concept in the early seventies. The women's movement had awakened a sleeping giant, and women flooded back onto campuses across the nation.

The rambling interview covered many subjects. We talked about Alverno's new teaching model and my experiences and responsibilities as president of the League. At the end of the meeting, Lois walked me to my car, shook my hand, and promised to be in touch. The interview had gone well, but it seemed more likely to result in a new friend than a new job. What experience did I have in interviewing, program development, or publications?

So I was surprised when Lois called me the following day. Could I meet with Sister Joel that afternoon? Wow. In the few hours before the meeting, I set out to learn all I could about Alverno. Without Google, the internet, or social media, my research consisted of a few frantic phone calls.

The college was founded in 1887 by the School Sisters of St. Francis, primarily to educate the sisters. Sister Joel, a history professor at Alverno, had been named president in 1968. Over and over, I heard the same message: "What Sister Joel Read is doing at Alverno is groundbreaking." I parked in front of the school that afternoon, my interest piqued, along with my anxiety level. *Lord, please don't let me embarrass myself.*

Lois's greeted me warmly, and together, we walked to the president's office. The amazing Sister Joel was a small woman with sharp features and penetrating eyes. Her dark hair was short and cut to fall straight around her face. Though a no-nonsense woman, she had a warm smile and a wry sense of humor. I liked her immediately.

The conversation was as relaxed and far-reaching as the day before—not like an interview at all. No one, including me, mentioned my lack of training or practical experience for the job's specifics. Sister Joel, like Lois, seemed more interested in my life experience and volunteer career. I left several hours later, buoyed by the energy of the discussion and grateful that fate had connected me with these two exceptional women. My lack of qualifications for the job in no way diminished my delight in learning about Alverno and meeting Sister Joel Reed and Lois Rice. I drove home determined to keep in touch with these women and follow the progress of Alverno and competence-based learning.

Thirteen

To my amazement, two days later, Lois called to offer me the position. Could I begin immediately? More astonishing, I would realize my goal of earning $1,000 a month, at least almost. There would be no work (or pay) for six weeks in the summer. That was fine with me—fewer sitters and more time with the kids.

If Chip was surprised by my ability to find a job, he didn't let on. He would now be in charge of getting the kids off to school in the morning, but his family responsibilities would stay the same. My workday, 7:30 a.m. to 3:30 p.m., required a 7:00 a.m. departure. However, it also got me home pretty close to the time the boys returned from school. Their lives would also be unchanged. Scotty already stayed for lunch at Shorewood Middle School, and Beav and Dann seemed okay with taking bag lunches to Lake Bluff Elementary.

It was Heather, my baby girl, who would bear the brunt of my decision to work. She cried when she learned the new job would keep me from being home when she came home from morning kindergarten each day. She would go home with a classmate whose mother had agreed to watch her after school.

My stomach churned while I got ready for work that first morning but more from excitement than fear. If Sister Joel and Lois thought I was up to the task, then surely they must know. More and more, it seemed this was the job for me.

It was two weeks before I learned what a miracle my hiring had been. Alverno's search for a coordinator of continuing education had been in the works for months. Applications had been closed and a field of ninety candidates whittled to a few finalists when Isabel first suggested my name. Ninety candidates! Knowing that would have terrified and tongue-tied me from the start. Somehow, by the grace of God, I had backed into a job for which I would never have applied at a school I'd barely heard of, requiring skills I didn't know I had. The interview process had lasted less than a week.

Working at Alverno was a joy from the start. Never had I been so stimulated by intellectual debate and new ideas. The college was and still is dedicated to educating women. Only recently have men been admitted and then only to master's programs. Though a product of women's education, I never thought much about it other than relishing the fact that there was no need to worry about hair and makeup during the week. The whole women's movement of the sixties had pretty much missed me. While some of my East Coast college friends became involved in marches and demonstrations, back in Milwaukee, I spent the sixties having babies, emulating the life of my mother, my grandmother, and my great-grandmother. If discussed at all in my crowd, we saw women's lib as a bunch of aggressive, unattractive women who probably couldn't get men of their own anyway. Why would women want to be equal to men? We had the vote. Let men earn a living and have their college sports. There was no endeavor nobler, thought I, than having babies and running a household.

That was all fine until it wasn't. The illusion that my world was secure had evaporated that day in the lawyer's office. Taking financial responsibility for myself was something I hadn't contemplated. Equal pay for equal work no longer sounded like a feminist rant. Just as competence-based learning made perfect sense, so too did the idea of educated women competing on a level playing field. My eyes opened to a new reality. The roles of women were changing, and it was time I reevaluated some long-held assumptions.

Fourteen

Alverno is known for its Women's Research Center. The director of the center, Kathy Gigl, was often called on to speak about women's issues. The more word spread about the center, the greater the demand for speakers. Kathy and I had become good friends almost immediately. Recognizing my burgeoning interest in the changing roles of women, she soon suggested I take on some of the speaking engagements. There was just one problem. I was terrified of public speaking.

That had not always been so. As president of the Junior League, I spoke regularly before audiences large and small. I enjoyed public speaking.

However, one day in April 1972, something strange happened to me. While delivering a year-end report at the annual spring luncheon, I suddenly felt faint. My hands began to sweat, my heart pounded, and my voice grew thin and shaky. The sounds around me, including my voice, faded as through in an echo chamber. I was terrified. It had come out of nowhere. Skipping the last two pages of my prepared remarks, I clung to the dais, mumbled a few words of thanks, and got off the stage as quickly as possible. *What on earth?* Digging my fingernails into my palms, I gulped air and tried to calm down while the vice president took the podium to deliver words of thanks and present me with a gift commemorating my two years as League president. By the time she was ready to present the gift, I had recovered enough to stand, smile, and mouth a weak thank you. Speaking would have been impossible. What was going on? On my way out, I cornered my friend Suzy and told her what happened. "Did I make a fool of myself?"

"I thought you got choked up saying goodbye to your board. No one noticed," Suzy assured me. "It sounds to me like you may have had a panic attack."

"But why?" I was dumbfounded. "Why all of a sudden? Why now?"

Several days later, my doctor agreed with Suzy's diagnosis but couldn't tell me why it happened or if it would happen again. Instead, he gave me a prescription for a mild sedative to take before future speaking engagements. Assuming my public speaking days were behind me, the pills went to the back of my medicine cabinet. It was not possible, however, to forget the horror of that day. Even the thought of standing at a podium made me feel faint.

A friend asked if I would say a few words to the new Junior League provisional class at a meeting in her home the following fall. No dais. No microphone. Just stand before a small gathering of women in a living room. I agreed without hesitation.

When the day came, I woke up feeling nervous but not panicky. I thought about the pills. There was no need to take one, I thought. Frankly, the potential effect of the pill terrified me more than speaking to a small group of women in a friend's living room.

But that afternoon, as the women settled down and the provisional chairman stood to introduce me, it happened again, the rapid heartbeat, the sweaty tingling, the echo of voices. If you have never experienced a panic attack, it is hard to grasp the sheer terror of the experience. I arose, clung to the back of a wingback chair, and somehow got through a truncated version of my remarks. How I managed is still a mystery. On the way home, I promised never to put myself in that position again. And the promise held—until now.

My array of excuses for refusing to help Kathy with speaking engagements began to sound flimsy, even to me. The time had come to share my secret. There had been no incidents since the provisional meeting, but there had been no opportunity for me to speak in public. My fear was still genuine.

Kathy understood as I knew she would. The challenge was how to get me before the public without having to call 911. Together, we developed a plan. The first try would be in a local south-side library with a small group of neighborhood women who wanted to know more about Alverno. We could sit around a table. For some reason, the idea of sitting was nonthreatening—much like a small meeting. Yes. I could do that. Not wanting to give me too much time to ponder the plan, Kathy scheduled my first group meeting for the next week. Eight women signed up.

At nine the morning of the meeting, we gathered in the community room of a small library near the college. After the women helped themselves to coffee, I had them use black Magic Markers to write their first names in large letters on each side of cardboard tents, made the night before from Chip's shirt cardboards. The women were primarily young and appeared to be shy and quiet. They did not seem to know one another.

"Let's start by going around the table. Please introduce yourself and share something you would like the group to know about you. I'll go first. I'm Carol Swallow, and I'm the coordinator of continuing education at Alverno College. I've lived in Milwaukee my whole life, but I'm new to this side of town."

Well, that went well, I thought. My heart pounded, but I was still upright. With a smile, I turned to the woman on my right. Slowly, one by one, each woman introduced herself. The first two said their names and recounted the names of their husbands and children. The third woman added her husband's occupation, and the rest followed suit. Not one of them said something personal about herself.

I looked around the table. "Do you realize each of you defined yourself by your husband and your children? Even by your husband's job? We still don't know a thing about you. Let's start again. This time tell us something about *you.*"

The second time around was better. Though it was evident that all eight women were homemakers, this time, we learned that Karen loved to sing, Mary hated ironing, and Lorraine was a Girl Scout leader. I relaxed. Soon I was speaking with the women, not to them. My heart stopped pounding.

"How many of you have thought about life after your last child goes to school all day?" I asked. There were chuckles as a few hands went up.

Somebody said, "Who hasn't?" More laughter.

"What about after your last child leaves home? How many of you have pictured your life then?"

More nervous laughter, but this time, no hands went up. It was apparent none of these women had thought beyond their child-rearing years. Not surprising. I hadn't either—before Alverno.

"Based on today's life expectancy for women," I continued, "we will live more than half of our lives after our children leave home. Too many of us have never imagined ourselves after child-rearing. I call that running out of script. Lots of attention focuses on helping men adjust to retirement. For men, running out of script happens around age sixty-five. But for you and me, 'retirement' may well start in our late thirties or early forties. What will you do for the rest of your lives?"

I had the women's attention. For the next half hour or so, I spoke with the group about the changing roles of women as comfortably as if I were in my living room, feeling none of the panic symptoms I so feared.

When it was time for questions and comments, the women—who had been so quiet when they arrived—were ready to participate. One by one, each opened up, shy at first, then bolder. By the time the session drew to a close, they had plans to meet again. These women were eager to identify their gifts, eager to develop skills, eager to follow their dreams. I was excited by the energy of the meeting and facing my fear of speaking.

Little by little, group by group, I moved from sitting to standing, from standing to a podium, from a podium to a dais. I graduated from speaking quietly to projecting my voice, to using a microphone. Inch by inch, my terrible fear of public speaking began to ebb. I would learn later that the fear of public speaking, or glossophobia, is a disorder many never conquer. Not that it was easy, because it was not. To this day, when facing an audience, my stomach goes flip-flop, and I take a breath and thank God for that miracle of healing so long ago. In the beautiful warm presence of the good School Sisters of Saint Francis, I grew in ways I had never imagined, and it felt good.

Fifteen

Kathy Gigl did far more than help me conquer my fear of speaking. She opened my eyes and my mind to the many issues facing women in the sixties and seventies. For the first time, the blessing of having a debt-free college education and the freedom to stay home with my babies was apparent. I could appreciate the remarkable difference an education would make in the women who came through my office. They were not looking to take over the world or a company ("glass ceiling" was not in our lexicon back then) but to gain some control over their own lives and futures.

Six months into the job, it was time to plan my first brochure of noncredit courses for the fall. Armed with new awareness, I gravitated toward classes that would expand women's horizons and help build their confidence. The Total Woman was the title of my first syllabus. It included courses such as Goals, Motivation, and Awareness (GMA), Training for Effectiveness, and I'd Rather Do It Myself.

GMA was an existing course designed to identify a woman's interests and strengths and help her set goals and map a course to achieve them. I'd Rather Do It Myself was a class to teach women how to handle minor repairs around the house. A handyman Chip and I had known for years agreed to come to Alverno and teach the course once a week for six weeks. On the final day, the class would meet at the home of one of the women to teach them to change fuses (no circuit breakers yet), check furnaces, and fix runny toilets, clogged garbage disposals, and so on. The title was a takeoff on a famous TV ad of the time that featured a mother peering over the shoulder of her adult daughter at the stove, telling her how to cook something (Minute Rice, I think). The daughter replies in an irritated voice, "Please, Mother, I'd rather do it myself."

Training for Effectiveness was another course suggested by Kathy. It was assertiveness training, but in 1973, assertiveness was an undesirable trait in women. Effectiveness was more appealing. When Kathy called on me to teach the class, I was not assertive enough to tell her I couldn't teach it. So, I ordered a primer on assertiveness training and set out to teach eight women, plus myself, the elusive art of being assertive.

To this day, I remember two rules: First, stand up for your rights without stepping on the other guy's (that would be aggression), and second, it is not necessary to be assertive in every situation. Both lessons have served me well.

It was a fun and challenging class. Along with guidelines, the book offered practice scenarios. One scenario stands out in my memory: You are walking through the grocery store when you run into a woman with whom you volunteer. You are fond of the woman and her husband and have seen them at a few social events, but your husband can't stand them. You hug and talk for a few minutes. Then she asks if you and your husband can come to dinner the following week.

Of course, you tell her how busy both your schedules are and thank her for asking.

"Oh, it doesn't have to be next week," she responds. "You pick a date that suits the two of you. We're pretty open."

Yikes. Now what? Of course, you will have to check your schedules, but you can't be busy for the rest of your lives. This situation calls for a no. Now, two-year-olds can and do say no with ease. Most men have little problem saying no. Women, on the other hand, find it more diffi-cult. The situation genuinely stumped the class. How to say no without hurting the woman's feelings? Quite naturally, they looked to me for the answer.

About to be exposed masquerading as a teacher, much less an as-sertive one, I suggested the women ponder the situation and come to the next class with suggested dialogues, keeping in mind our previous lessons. Mercifully, we moved on to another topic until class was over.

As soon as everyone left, I dashed to the Women's Research Center to pose the question to my assertive friend Kathy.

"Being honest with her would be rude," I moaned. "There will never be a good time to have dinner with this couple. Help."

Together, we came up with this: "That is so nice of you, but I'm afraid I will have to say no. With the kids' activities and both of us working full-time, we have agreed to scale back our social activities to spend more time together as a family. I hope you understand."

You have said no upfront without hurting her feelings. And it would take a pretty aggressive woman to say she didn't understand such a noble endeavor. There was but one teensy problem. You and your husband have never discussed such an agreement. The group agreed that a little white lie was far superior to devastating the woman by telling the unvarnished truth. And besides, we agreed it sounded like something we all should discuss with our husbands.

Training for Effectiveness became one of the most popular noncredit courses in the continuing ed program. Soon Kathy and I both led classes. Each new group brought new challenges; each group taught me as much or more than I taught them. Little by little, I acquired a tool that would be of value throughout my life. Am I good at saying no today? Not always. I still worry about hurting feelings. But I know the difference between assertive and aggressive behavior; therein lies the lesson.

Sixteen

The summer of 1974 was a summer of change. We had sold our beautiful home on Pine Lake in the spring. Not to worry. Chip's grandparents' old summer cottage sat empty at the far end of the lake. To me, the cottage was dark and more than a little spooky. The whole place smelled of mildew and old memories. If the kids didn't love Pine Lake so much, I would have pushed harder to stay in town that summer. But I didn't have the heart.

More than our address changed that summer. I changed too. While Chip and the kids dove back into life at Pine Lake without missing a beat, I experienced a growing sense of unease. My work at Alverno introduced me to a different world, where hard work and determination, not power and influence, earned privilege and success. Suddenly, life in this enclave of affluence and tradition felt like a merry-go-round, and I no longer had a ticket to ride.

"How can you be unhappy in such a beautiful place?" my mom would ask.

Chip and I argued about almost everything that summer, as much my fault as his. It seemed neither of us had tolerance for the noise and chaos of four active children, even our own. Weekends were marginally better. For the first time since we married, I didn't crew for Chip on our E-boat, a twenty-eight-foot inland scow we raced on weekends and in regattas. The free time gave me more time with the kids and eliminated the inherent tensions between skipper and crew.

The first weeks of that summer, I still worked. It proved a blessed relief from the problems at home. The quiet of the forty-minute commute was restorative and the challenges of the job all-consuming. My weeks off in July and August flew by, filled with picnics, sailboat races, and cookouts.

Toward the end of August, as I prepared to start work again and our summer babysitter headed back to high school, Chip suggested taking the children on a boat trip up the Mississippi. It seemed the perfect answer. He did this kind of thing best, and the boys were old enough to help with Heather. What a sight they made pulling out of the driveway that August morning, arms waving goodbye out the back window of the station wagon, the motorboat packed with gear trailing behind.

Shortly after they returned from the Mississippi, Scotty began to complain of backaches. I scolded him for scrunching down in the back of the car, reading comic books. "Sit up straight," I told him, "and your back won't ache." It didn't occur to any of us that his backaches were more than the typical growing pains of a thirteen-year-old boy.

Seventeen

Moving back to town brought a certain solace. For the first time, all four kids were in school all day. My volunteer work had always kept me busy but not every minute of every hour of every day. Being a mother who worked outside the home brought a whole new set of challenges. And yet, I loved my work—the way it stretched my mind in new and exciting ways. And it felt good to help feed and clothe our family.

Meanwhile, Chip's financial problems continued to escalate. On top of everything, Ausblick Ski Club, in its fourth season, was in financial trouble. Whether membership dues alone could have supported the club as planned, we will never know because the original budget did not include purchasing snowmaking equipment, a luxury found at large ski resorts. Wisconsin weather is notoriously unpredictable. It gets cold enough, but whether the cold will produce snow is less certain. Chip decided that using snowmaking equipment at Ausblick would guarantee members got their money's worth. It was a good idea.

Then he had a brainstorm. As long as he bought snow machines for Ausblick, why not buy enough to sell to other ski hills for a profit? The premise was sound, except for one thing. He failed to arrange financing to cover the gap between paying the manufacturer and collecting from the ski hills. "Not a problem," Chip figured. His rental properties brought in plenty. He could borrow money from the rent collection and repay it when he got paid for the machines. I don't know whether he knew this was "comingling" funds, but the government did.

I was not proud of the person I became during those terrible days, not the wife, not the mother, not the friend. Those who had been close to me, many since childhood, grew farther and farther away. Sewing Club, the women with whom I had once shared everything, continued to rotate houses for their monthly meetings, but my limited lunch hour allowed little time for a round trip to the east side, much less time to visit and sew. Bombarded by fear, stress, and uncertainty, I became irritable and angry.

Meanwhile, Chip fell back into the habit of stopping for a drink after work at the MAC or some other local watering hole. Most nights, I fed the children early because they couldn't wait until 7:00 p.m. for dinner. Chip and I would then have dinner later. Thursday nights, however, we had started a tradition called family dinner. On Thursdays, I served dinner in the dining room on the good china, complete with cloth napkins and candlelight. I intended it as a time to practice manners and polite conversation. We accomplished neither. By the time Chip got home, he had been drinking, and the children were hungry and bickering. Often, the food was overcooked or cold. Ever the martyr, I punished us by herding the group into the dining room for family dinner. More often than not, Chip came down hard on one of the boys for some minor infraction, sending him from the table in tears. Our family was falling apart, and I was part of the problem.

One evening, Chip came home in a horrid mood. He fixed a drink and headed for the living room, grunting at Danny and Heather, who were lying on the floor in the den watching cartoons. It was not a good night to report another summons, but so be it. He was furious—first at the news and then at the messenger. But this time, I was as angry as he.

"What have you done now?" I yelled. "Is there anyone in Milwaukee who doesn't want to sue you?"

It might have been wiser to wait for a time when Chip hadn't been drinking, but when was that? Tired and disgusted, I was just getting started. Details of the argument remain vague, except the end when Chip grabbed his car keys and headed for the garage.

"This is never going to work!" he shouted over his shoulder. "I'm outta here."

It wasn't the first time the kids had heard us fight, but never had he slammed out like that. Heather began to cry, and Beav and Scotty came down from upstairs.

"What happened?"

"Why did Dad leave?"

"Why is he so mad?"

"When will he come home?"

I did my best to answer their questions and assured them their dad loved them very much. It was me he was mad at—sometimes moms and dads did not get along. It was hours before they were all tucked into bed, each praying their dad would come home soon.

Sometime before dawn, Chip came home and slipped into bed quietly, indicating he had not continued to drink after he left. At least he would be there to get the kids off to school in the morning. Pretending to be asleep, I moved closer to the wall.

I staggered out of bed in the morning and reset the alarm to wake Chip at seven thirty. The kids would be so happy. God had answered their prayers—Dad was home.

Eighteen

Heather and I got home around four thirty the next afternoon to find Chip in the front yard throwing a football with the boys. My heart sank. I'd been jumpy all day, fueled by lack of sleep and a sick feeling that I had no control over my life. Other than Chip coming home early, the evening progressed much like any other. The very normalcy depressed me. Once again, a curtain dropped on an ugly scene as though it never happened. Nothing would change. It never did.

Early the following day, Chip rolled over and pulled me toward him. It was a familiar pattern, one I had begun to loathe. As if intimacy could ease the pain of the love we had lost. The thin veneer of anger beneath the surface of our relationship had diminished our ability to please one another. Afterward, neither was inclined to offer words of comfort or forgiveness; we each thought our own thoughts. The joyless act left me empty and feeling not a little sorry for myself.

"We should get separated." Chip's voice was flat, not angry.

I came back to the present with a start. Despite the depth of my unhappiness, the thought of separating had never occurred to me. No one in the seventies separated—at least not the people we knew. They bucked up and soldiered on, as had their parents and grandparents before them. Wallowing in my misery had made me blind to the fact that Chip was equally miserable. He swung his legs over the side of the bed, still talking.

"I can get an apartment downtown. My lawyer can draw up legal separation papers this afternoon." Separating was not a spur-of-the-moment decision.

"Fine with me," I snapped. "Shouldn't I have a lawyer?"

He headed for the shower.

"That's up to you. I'll meet you downtown at two."

When I heard his car pull out of the garage, I closed the bedroom door and dialed my friend Susy. Her husband Dave was a lawyer. Susy and I had shared our lives since fifth grade. We spent hours in Pheasant Hollow, our name for a stand of weeping willows near her house, dreaming of futures filled with love and romance. While we were rooming together our senior year at the University of Wisconsin, Susy met Dave, a law student who played the ukulele and took her on picnics. When Chip and I dated later in the year, the four of us spent a lot of time together. We had been in each other's weddings. Aside from being a longtime friend, Dave was the only lawyer I knew to call. After listening to my sob story, Susy put Dave on the phone. He agreed to go with me to the meeting but wanted to see me in his office beforehand. Our neighbor Alice agreed to keep an eye on the kids for the afternoon.

Shortly before 1:00 p.m., I parked my car at the MAC parking lot and walked the few blocks to Dave's office. The fresh air and exercise helped clear my head. What were we doing? I understood why an apartment downtown would appeal to Chip. He could come and go as he pleased, entertain whom he chose, and avoid the chaos and responsibility of day-to-day life with four active children. More to the point, he could get away from me. That made sense too. Even I wanted to get away from me. Wherever the blame lay, however justified my anger, I found the pain of rejection devastating.

Large windows that overlooked the street bathed David's office in light. He was waiting for me. It felt strange to sit there, across his desk, lawyer and client. As I poured out the litany of ways Chip had wronged me, he took notes on a yellow legal pad and listened carefully, without judgment. Finally, he put down the pad and looked at his watch.

"Before we go, let me ask you something." He laid his pencil across his pad and looked at me. "Where do you want to be a year from now?"

Wow. Had he asked me where I thought I would be a year from then, the answer would have been easy. But this was a different question, one that implied choice.

"Not married to Chip." The words surprised us both, but I knew they were true the minute they left my mouth. I wanted an end to the chaos, the fighting, the broken promises, the abusive behavior, the constant worry, and the alcohol-fused unreliability. Life needed to change for all of us, and that wouldn't happen without significant changes. Having no control over a future that affected us all was exasperating. Just eleven months ago, Chip had laughed at my ability to find a job, to make a difference. But he was wrong. A year ago, the thought of supporting the kids by myself would have panicked me. Now I knew it was possible.

"Well then, let's go," Dave said, reaching for our coats.

To this day, I am grateful for Dave's patience and professionalism in the face of what must have been difficult for him. Neither of us could know how profoundly the question he asked would change my life and those of our children.

The three men exchanged handshakes when we entered the conference room. Chip's lawyer closed the door and took a seat at the head of the table with Chip on his left. Dave and I sat across from Chip. The lawyer leaned back in his chair and opened a thin file in front of him.

"We are here to draw up an agreement for a legal separation," he said. "This should be fairly simple." He pushed some papers across the shiny table toward Dave. Dave didn't move.

"My client does not want a separation," Dave said.

The man continued, unfazed. "It's just a trial separation. Chip is living under tremendous stress right now, and he needs—they need—some time to sort things out."

"My client doesn't want a separation," Dave repeated. "She wants a divorce."

The startling words hung in the room. Chip tapped the eraser of his pencil on the table in a nervous drumbeat, not looking up.

"Is that right, Carol?" the lawyer asked.

"It is," I said, the words echoing in the big room.

"In that case, Chip will want a divorce lawyer," he said. "I will recommend someone to take it from here."

Within a week, a tough divorce lawyer from the firm took over the case. The battle was joined.

Nineteen

As it turned out, the freedom of living in an apartment downtown lost its appeal when Chip was facing a divorce rather than a separation. An apartment would be too expensive, he said. He would move to the guest room. His new lawyer called the shots now, and abandoning the domicile was not in their game plan.

In 1975, there was no such thing as a no-fault divorce in Wisconsin. Even if a divorce was amicable, the law required that one spouse sue the other "for cause" and prove the claim in court.

I sued Chip for irreconcilable differences. Sadly, being miserable was not considered an irreconcilable difference. I would have to be more specific, describing specific dates and details of verbal and physical abuse incidents. It would be painful. There were plenty of examples, but it was not my intent to ruin Chip. He was our children's father, after all. My goal was to control my life and free our kids of the poisonous atmosphere created by constant bickering and ugly confrontations.

Chip didn't see it that way. Chaos had filled his home life as a child. He and his sister, Susy, had grown up with an alcoholic father and an emotionally unstable mother who managed the challenges of child-rearing by sending them away. Chip was shipped off to prep school in Connecticut early on, followed by eight weeks of camp in the summer. Those scars still ran deep in him. I wanted more for our children.

The stress of living under the same roof was enormous. At times, Chip arrived home from work drunk, sarcastic, and loaded for bear.

Often I was the lone target of his derision but not always. One Saturday, Chip came in shouting for all of us to come to the living room.

"What do we want more than anything?" he shouted.

The kids shrank into the sofa. I knew better than to interrupt.

"We want Mommy and Daddy to stay together. That's what we want. Isn't it?"

Scotty nodded. Heather began to cry. Steve and Danny were silent, staring at their dad.

"Chip, please …" I pleaded.

"That's what I want too. It's Mom who doesn't want that. She doesn't want us to be together. Do you, Mom? Do you?"

"That's not fair!" I yelled. "Leave the children out of this." How could I answer his accusation without maligning their dad? Our children loved their dad. They didn't understand the man who sat there, angry and attacking their mom.

This had to stop. I went upstairs and called Dave.

Within weeks, we appeared before a judge who ordered Chip to vacate the premises. At the same time, he appointed a guardian ad litem to act "in the best interest of the children." I do not know why it had not occurred to me that Chip would fight for custody of Scotty, Beav, Danny, and Heather. He loved them every bit as much. In my mind, the very reasons for the divorce—Chip's drinking and irresponsible behavior—would disqualify him as a legal guardian. Now a court-appointed stranger was to meet with us a few times and make custody recommendations to the court? That was nuts.

And so our marriage and the vows we had made so sincerely, if naively, just fourteen years before unraveled. Finally accepting the fact, Chip took a new tack. He filed for personal bankruptcy. As fall turned into winter, there was much to be done at the ski hill to get ready for the ski season, so the children spent many weekends with their dad working on the hill and spending nights with Granny at Pine Lake.

I welcomed uninterrupted time to run errands and do chores on the weekends, but the silence was deafening. Occasionally, a friend would include me in a dinner party. While I appreciated the kindness, more often than not, the evenings were awkward. Conversations with people I'd known all my life became strained as they tried to avoid subjects that might make me uneasy. As a result, we danced around the elephant in the living room until it was time for me to retreat. Often I felt more alone than if I had stayed home.

Twenty

As deeply conflicted and lonesome as my personal life had become, I felt valued and supported at work. Through it all, Alverno was my island of peace.

One morning in early January, Scotty came dragging into my bedroom and threw himself on the bed. It was almost 7:00 a.m. Over the past three months, the kids and I had worked out a routine of sorts, still shaky but functional.

"Not again," I moaned and felt his forehead. I reached for the thermometer. He'd been in and out of school since before Christmas, feeling lousy and running a low-grade fever. Despite our doctor's assurance that there was "a lot of this going around," I was at my wit's end.

When the little silver line crept past one hundred, I sighed, picked up the phone, and dialed. Our pediatrician had been with us since Scotty was born. Everyone loved him. Not only was he accessible, but he was a great cheerleader for tired moms. Fortunately, in thirteen years as his patients, there had been little reason for me to call on him beyond routine check-ups. Until now. When his wife answered, I apologized for the early call. She assured me it was no trouble.

"Scotty's fever is back," I said when he picked up. "And his back still aches. Should we try a blood test?"

"Well, if his back continues to ache, perhaps you should call an orthopedic doctor? I doubt the fever is a problem, but perhaps you might get to the root of his back pain. I'll check back with you in a few days." With that, he was gone.

Dr. Mike Kubly was a popular orthopedist in Milwaukee. I caught him at home and explained the situation. When he heard I would be at work all day, he suggested I meet him in the ER at Columbia Hospital after work.

Mike was waiting when we got there that afternoon. He and his wife, Billie, were members of Ausblick Ski Club, and our families skied together often. He had seen me for intermittent back problems over the years. We had not seen one another since Chip and I separated, so I was grateful for his warm greeting.

He began by asking Scotty to tell him what was going on. Scotty told him about the backaches and being tired all the time. I explained his recurring fevers and my frustration at not being taken seriously.

"I'm not a hysterical mother, Mike. Something is wrong with Scotty. I feel it in my bones."

Mike listened carefully and took his time with the examination. Then he turned to me.

"I'd like to keep him here for a day or two," he said. "It will give us time to run some tests. Don't worry, Carol, we'll get to the bottom of this." Scotty and I agreed with the plan. He just wanted to feel better.

The following day, they called in a rheumatologist, concerned Scotty might have rheumatoid arthritis. I couldn't sleep that night, waiting for the tests to come back. Rheumatoid arthritis was a crippling and painful disease, more often associated with adults. Surely he didn't have something that serious. To our relief, the tests came back negative. The novelty of the hospital had worn off, and he was eager to get home. He said he felt fine, but the nagging fever was still there. I pleaded with him to be patient. We would know something soon.

The next day, Mike asked if I knew Dr. Richard Fritz.

"Sure. He's my internist."

"I would like it if he would stop in and see Scotty," Mike said.

I called Dick at home that evening, surprised when he seemed to hesitate at my request.

"I don't normally work with children, Carol, but I'll give Mike a call and try to see Scotty tomorrow when I'm at the hospital."

I didn't know then that Dick Fritz was an oncologist as well as an internist. I just knew I was comforted because someone had listened. The doctors were doing their best to determine what sapped Scotty's strength and caused the continuous fevers and backaches.

Twenty-one

It was still dark when I swung into the empty parking lot at Alverno that Friday. Scotty's hospital stay had put me behind in my work. I looked forward to some quiet time to catch up. The students wouldn't arrive for another hour or so. Most of the faculty were nuns who walked over from St. Joseph convent, a beautiful stone building nestled in a wooded area at the far corner of the campus. A cold winter wind whipped the bare tree branches in a crazy dance that made the convent windows twinkle like Christmas tree lights. I lingered in the warm car, humming along as Karen Carpenter sang my favorite song, "Top of the World." Her voice flowed from the speakers like lava, mellow and soothing. Fifteen months ago, Alverno College was unknown to me, and now I was the coordinator of continuing education. It felt as unreal as it had that first day.

Sisters Joel Read and Georgine Loacker made their way toward the administration building deep in conversation, heads bowed against the cold. How little these brilliant women resembled the nuns of my youth. Since Vatican II, it seemed the only difference between the nuns and lay faculty was a dash of lipstick. Sometimes not even that.

The administration building loomed in front of me, an ugly yellowish brick structure built in the 1950s. While the ancient stone convent had charm, the admin building was utterly devoid of character. For a religion with such ornate churches, plain appeared the watchword for many Catholic institutions.

I grabbed my briefcase and headed toward the door. To my surprise, lights were already on in the admissions department. Mary, our twenty-six-year-old financial aid guru, looked up from her desk.

"I'm impressed," I said.

"Don't be." She laughed. "My husband needed the car, so he dropped me off on his way to work. You're early yourself. How's Scotty?"

"He's doing okay, just eager to get home," I said. "Gotta run. The spring brochure goes to print today."

My office was austere, like the rest of the building, but I couldn't complain. It was one of only a few private offices in the department, complete with a door, two windows, a desk, and a semigracious seating area for student interviews. A Christmas poinsettia was gasping its last on the wide windowsill, next to a family photo of me with Scotty, Beav, Danny, and Heather on Vail Mountain. Could that have been just a year ago?

I closed my door, picked up the phone, and dialed home. The job of getting the kids off to school had fallen to eleven-year-old Beav this week. Hardly ideal, but the best I could come up with on short notice. What had started as a day or two hospital stay for Scotty had stretched to five days. Once Beav assured me all was well, I closed my door and got to work.

The morning flew, consumed by details of the massive cut-and-paste job that would be Alverno's spring continuing education brochure. There were no computer software programs to guide me through the layout process. PCs and MACs were luxuries of future generations.

Shortly after lunch, there was a soft knock. Our receptionist, Lynn, poked in her head.

"It's Dr. Fritz's office."

I grabbed the receiver, wiping paste from my fingers.

"Dick?"

A woman's voice asked me to hold for the doctor.

It was about time. The doctors had run tests all week, and I wanted some results. Scotty was tired of being in the hospital, and I was nearly at the end of my rope juggling job, sitters, the bits and pieces of our ugly divorce, and now Scotty's hospital stay. My pen tapped impatiently on the edge of the desk as I gazed out the window at the bare trees and gray sky.

Dick finally picked up. His voice was serious. "We got some test results today, Carol." A pause. "Scotty's bone marrow biopsy shows malignant cells in his bone marrow."

The room tilted. *Malignant cells?* The words terrified me. Two days ago, the doctors suspected Scotty might have rheumatoid arthritis, and I'd agonized all night about the effect of such a debilitating disease on an active teenager. But no one had even whispered the word *malignant*.

The receiver felt like an anvil in my hand. A sound like the ocean roared through my head. It was hard to breathe. Laying my cheek on the cool metal surface of the desk, I wondered if I would faint.

"Do you mean malignant as in cancer?" I whispered.

"I'm afraid so."

Today, more than forty years later, cancer is no longer thought of as a death knell. Many cancers today are treatable, even curable. That was not the case in 1975. No diagnosis struck greater fear in the hearts of patients and their families. The diagnosis couldn't be correct.

Dick went on to describe the various test results and their implications. He assured me there were breakthroughs in cancer research every day. It was hard for me to follow what he said. It occurred to me later that the brain can only process so much before it shuts down. I felt the door closing on my sanity.

"Could he die?" My voice was weak.

Dick didn't mince words. He was an oncologist, and he knew the odds.

"He could, yes."

He went on. We would begin treatment as soon as possible. Could Scotty be at his office early next week? For now, there was no reason to keep him in the hospital another night. Dick would sign the release for me to pick him up after work.

"But what will I tell him?" I breathed. "What can I possibly tell him?"

My concern at that moment focused on 5:00 p.m. when I would pick him up. How could Scotty understand what I couldn't grasp? Indeed the word *cancer* would frighten him as it had me. I needed time, just as he would need time, to digest the reality and implications of such a diagnosis.

Dick understood.

"We needn't use the word *cancer* at this point," he said. "I'll stop by and tell him he can go home today, and you'll bring him to the office next week for a shot."

If there was more to that conversation, I have forgotten. Never before or since have I felt more devastated or alone. Trying to wrap my head around this frightening news terrified me.

Somehow the rest of the afternoon went by. I gathered the scattered pieces of my spring brochure and phoned the printer, who agreed to give me some leeway on the due date. Like a zombie, I cleaned up my desk. I dreaded calling Chip as though saying the diagnosis out loud would make it more real. It seemed every conversation we had these days was fraught with anger and mistrust.

Chip didn't believe me at first. He thought it was some cruel joke meant to scare him. It could not be that serious, he said. My overreaction was typical. He would call Dick Fritz himself. With that, he hung up.

It was dark by the time I pulled into the hospital parking lot, sick and scared. It never occurred to me that Scotty wouldn't get better, just as it never occurred to him. My precious baby was only thirteen years old. His life had just begun. How could I look at him without my heart breaking? I closed my eyes, bowed my head, and pleaded for God to give me strength, to help me through this next hour.

In Scotty's room, the television was on. He laughed at a Rocky and Bullwinkle cartoon. "Moot and quirrel" is what he called them when he was little and sat on his pint-sized red chair in front of the television. I bent over and kissed his forehead.

"Hi, Mom," he said, still looking at the TV. "Did you hear? Dr. Fritz says I can go home."

"Well then, let's grab your things and get out of here."

His clothes were in the closet where we had hung them five days earlier when we thought a day or two of tests would get to the root of the problem. If only I hadn't pushed so hard, the kids and I might be home now, laughing and talking around the kitchen table, eating homemade pizza, and planning for their weekend ski outing with their dad. We wouldn't know the scary truth, at least not yet. If only we could turn back the clock.

Twenty-two

We got through the next few weeks somehow. My mother and the few close friends with whom I shared the diagnosis were devastated. Chip's mother was angry, of course. She was confident I had the facts wrong. But Chip, like I, was numb. Meanwhile, Scotty felt better again and had returned to school.

One afternoon while I folded laundry on my bed after work, Scotty and two of the neighborhood boys pounded up the stairs and into my room, out of breath. He grabbed a rolled-up pair of socks from the laundry pile and began to shoot buckets at a phantom hoop. His back was to me when he said, "Mom, do I have cancer?"

I froze. News travels fast, but bad news travels faster. Looking back, I realize he probably heard something from one of his friends who had overheard something at home. No matter. The time had come.

"Cancer is a big word for a lot of things, sweetheart. We see Dr. Fritz tomorrow. Let's talk with him about it."

"Okay," Scotty agreed as he and his friends took off for his bedroom.

After the children were in bed, I dialed Dick at home. He answered on the first ring.

"Scotty knows he has cancer," I said. "He's going to ask you about it tomorrow."

"Then I guess it's time." His voice was kind.

Doctors are much more direct with patients today. In the 1970s, it was not uncommon for a doctor or a parent to try to spare a patient from the frightening reality of a potentially fatal diagnosis, especially if that patient was a child.

The next afternoon, after he had drawn blood and given Scotty a shot, Dr. Fritz asked if he had any questions.

"Do I have cancer?" Scotty asked without hesitation.

Dick's voice was gentle. "Yes, Scotty, you do have a form of cancer."

I looked out the window, dreading the moment, but now I turned toward my son. He made no sound, but tears were streaming down his beautiful cheeks. Just when I thought my heart could break no more, it cracked wide open and scattered my last bits of courage onto the examining room floor.

"We hope the medicine in the shots I am giving will help kill the malignant cells," Dick continued.

"What if that doesn't work?" asked Scotty, echoing the question I was too frightened to ask.

"Then we shall try something else," Dick responded. "Cancer research is uncovering new treatments every day. Meanwhile, I'll see you next week." He put his hand out and shook Scotty's hand and then mine.

So that was it. The dreaded moment was behind us. Scotty knew. However, if anything, the road ahead seemed more daunting. The bankruptcy moved ahead, and it was only a matter of time until our house would go on the market. When extreme cold froze the pipes in the back of the house, there was no money for plumbers, so Chip came over and turned off the water to the back bathroom.

Mother Swallow sent a moving van to pick up the many treasures she had "loaned" us over the years, including paintings, oriental rugs, and a beautiful dining room set with twelve matching chairs that had belonged to Chip's grandmother. I didn't object for the same reasons I sought no alimony—pride and an uncomfortable feeling that somehow I was at fault for the failure of our marriage.

Twenty-three

It was noon, and Heather and I were hungry. The boys were with their dad, and we had run errands all morning. As we walked past the McDonald's on Oakland Avenue, the door burst open, and a group of teenagers spilled onto the sidewalk, followed by a cloud of mouth-watering french-fry smells. I didn't dare stop. Heather was the only child in America who wouldn't eat at McDonald's. Ever since the day she threw up a Big Mac all over her lunch tray, and her brothers made a major scene of being grossed out, she had refused to eat there. I understood, but it certainly was inconvenient at times. I was astonished when she stopped and said, "Let's go to McDonald's."

"Are you sure?" I asked. She nodded. "Well then, let's go."

Maybe it was because this was a different McDonald's, or maybe it was because the boys weren't with us, but Heather polished off a Big Mac and fries without hesitation or repercussions; thank you, Lord. As we rose to leave, someone called my name. Sarah Barnes, a young woman I knew from my volunteer life, came toward us. She worked for Barkin, Herman, Solochek, and Paulsen, the largest public relations firm in Wisconsin, handling much of their pro bono work. Our paths often crossed over the years. Just last spring, we spent hours together when I cochaired the 1974 Lakefront Festival of Arts. She was attractive, fun, and competent. We hugged, and I introduced her to Heather.

"How's life at Alverno these days?"

"Going well. The continuing ed program is growing so fast it's hard to keep up. I love Alverno and my job, but I'm afraid I will have to find something that pays better."

Why did I say that? It wasn't something I'd seriously contemplated. But it was true. Alverno paid me nine months of the year, even though I worked an extra month to meet my brochure deadlines. What had seemed the perfect job when Chip and I were together had become more and more difficult. The fact was, I could no longer afford the luxury of summers without a paycheck.

"How are things at Barkin Herman?"

"Crazy busy. We are just weeks away from the Lakefront Festival, and you know how that is. I have more work than I can handle." She paused. "You might be the perfect person to help me out. You know many of the clients we work with, and you certainly know the newspapers and reporters who cover the nonprofits. Let me talk to Norm. He likes you, and he knows I need help. Maybe we can hire you at Barkin Herman."

Norm Paulsen was Sarah's boss and the managing partner of Barkin, Herman, Solochek, and Paulsen. Because of his vast connections and knowledge of the Milwaukee community, he was one of the first people recommended for me to see when my job search began. He had met with me for the better part of an hour and promised to keep me in mind if he heard of anything. But nothing ever came of it. I didn't know much about public relations, but then what had I known about continuing education or Alverno, for that matter? Working with Sarah would be a treat, and the Barkin Herman offices were in downtown Milwaukee, a good fifteen minutes closer to Shorewood, where I hoped to live.

"That would be great," I said, hugging her.

"We'll stay in touch. Nice to meet you, Heather." With a wave, she disappeared around the corner.

"How do you feel?" I asked Heather.

"Good," she said. "I think I like McDonald's now." And just like that, in the most unlikely of places, in the most improbable way, another door had opened.

Twenty-four

I found myself fantasizing about working at Barkin Herman. The more I thought about it, the more appealing it sounded, and the more anxious I became. Had Sarah forgotten? Had she thought better of it? Had Norm balked at my inexperience? Of course, he had. Why would he take a chance on someone with no experience in public relations?

Just as I convinced myself I was fatally flawed, Sarah called and suggested we meet the following Monday afternoon at the firm's offices in the First Wisconsin Bank Center. My emotions ping-ponged between confidence and self-doubt all weekend. Any self-assurance I'd gained at Alverno faded fast.

By Monday, I was a wreck. Going to work was difficult, but staying home would have been worse. I knew Norm was a wonderful, kind man. It was hardly a trip into the lion's den. Either I was suitable for this job, or I wasn't. Simple as that.

As I headed toward downtown on I-94, the spectacle of the towering First Wisconsin Center, silhouetted against the sunlit beauty of Lake Michigan, was breathtaking. Having grown up on the bluffs of Lake Michigan, I was used to the lake's ever-changing colors and moods. Today, it was at its best—sparkling with hope.

The new forty-floor First Wisconsin Center was the closest thing to a skyscraper Milwaukee could boast. The difference between the Catholic simplicity of Alverno and the opulence of this bastion of corporate America was stunning. This "for-profit" world intimidated as well as intoxicated.

The cadence of my high heels clicking on the alabaster floors of the lobby seemed to say, "You can do this. You can do this. You can do this."

On the twentieth floor, I entered a large double door with a sign reading simply "Barkin Herman Solochek & Paulsen."

The elegant waiting area was windowless, bathed in soft, ambient lighting. A massive desk sat in the middle of the space. It was uncluttered except for a telephone with a bank of buttons, all seeming to blink at once. A beautifully coiffed receptionist raised a polished fingernail as she put a caller on hold.

"You must be Carol Swallow," she said. "Sarah will be with you in a moment. Please have a seat."

"Carol, it's so good to see you." Sarah stepped out of the office behind the receptionist and rounded the desk, her hand outstretched. At the last minute, she withdrew her hand in favor of a hug. I was grateful.

"Come with me. We're in Norm's office," she said and headed back the way she had come.

The office was impressive. An expanse of floor-to-ceiling windows looked out over the deep blue lake dotted with tiny white sails. The four men seated there rose to their feet as we came in.

"Carol, this is Barney Solochek, Dave Herman, and Joe Stadola." Sarah gestured toward each in turn. "You know Norm. Everybody, this is Carol Swallow." They motioned us toward the empty couch. Norm opened the conversation. He was as genuine as I remembered. So were Barney, Dave, and Joe. Gratefully, they seemed more interested in my volunteer experience than in my understanding of public relations. I felt at ease, and the interview flew by. I asked questions too and was surprised to learn that Sarah was the only woman besides the secretaries in the thirty-member firm. "The last of the great paternal organizations," Sarah quipped. The men laughed. As a product of women's education and a student of women's issues for the past two and a half years, I thought this would be quite a change.

When our conversation drew to a close, Norm suggested we step down the hall to the corner office to meet Ben Barkin, creator and founder of the firm. Of course I knew who Ben Barkin was. Everyone in Milwaukee knew who Ben Barkin was. He was larger than life, befriending the little guy and the rich and famous in equal measure. I stood in the doorway as Norm introduced us. Ben stopped what he was doing and came around his desk to take my hand. The warmth of his smile assured me there was no one he would rather be meeting at that moment. *Wow*, I thought. No wonder this guy is such a success. A google search could have told me he was named "best publicist in the country" just a few years earlier.

The meeting over, Norm walked me to the elevator, promising to be in touch. I floated through the lobby, excited by the new opportunity and the prospect of earning a living wage. We hadn't talked specifics, but the firm's reputation and the elegance of the offices indicated the salary would surely be more than what I was earning at Alverno. That was my goal, after all. At that moment, however, I would have paid them for the privilege of working there.

As the week went by without a word, it was hard to concentrate on work. I found myself avoiding or postponing meetings, filled with the guilty secret that I might not be there to carry out the proposed plans. Friday afternoon, after closing my office door and saying a quick prayer, I picked up the phone and called Norm's office. "Who's calling, please?" asked the receptionist when I asked for Norm.

"It's Carol Swallow," I said.

"Let me see if he's available, Carol."

Oh, help. Now I've done it. Norm said he would be in touch with me. Of course, he won't be available. Do I dare hang up?

"Hello, Carol." Norm's voice caught me off guard.

"I was just wondering if you had made any decision about hiring me," I blurted.

Norm paused and then laughed. "Not yet. Barney has been out of the office for a few days and won't be in until Monday."

"Will you know any more on Monday than you know now?" I

countered. My cheeks were flaming. What on earth had come over me? The stress of the last few months had finally sent me over the edge.

There was silence on the other end of the line. I wanted to die.

Years later, in a Wayne Dwyer secret power of negotiating class, I learned that once an offer is on the table, the first person who speaks loses. But I didn't know that then. I was too horrified at myself to speak.

"You're probably right about that." Norm chuckled finally. "Why don't you come in around five? We'll talk."

I let out the breath I had been holding.

"Perfect. See you then." I hung up the phone and rocked back in my desk chair, shocked by what had just occurred. It was totally out of character for me. Either I had done the stupidest thing in my life or the smartest. Only time would tell.

Twenty-five

Getting downtown by five would be a challenge. The kids were going to Pine Lake for the weekend. I called Chip, and he agreed to get Heather from the sitter. Then the sitter agreed Heather could stay until Chip came. And last was a call to our neighbor Alice to ask if she would tell the boys to be ready when their dad picked them up at five thirty and not to forget Heather's overnight bag, which was in the front hall. By the time the arrangements were made, there was just enough time to make it to Norm's office on time.

Connie was still at the front desk when I arrived, looking as fresh and professional, no doubt, as she had eight hours ago. This time, she recognized me. Norm was waiting. I could go right in.

Norm came around his desk to shake my hand, and then he returned to his desk chair and motioned for me to take one of the chairs across from him. When I was settled, he leaned back in his chair and made a tent with his fingers, tapping them against his chin. It was just the two of us. This time, there was no small talk.

"As you may know, Schlitz Brewing Company is a major client of this firm," he began. "Over the ten years Schlitz sponsored the Great Circus Parade in Milwaukee, Barkin Herman took on as many as twenty additional employees. The area of empty desks you saw across from Sarah's office was the Circus Parade bullpen, bustling with activity year-round. Those employees did nothing but work on the parade. When Schlitz decided to drop the event last year, we were faced with letting go almost all those people. It was a difficult time."

"I can imagine," I said, trying to sound sympathetic though my stomach was sinking. Of course they would not want to take on someone new if they had just eliminated so many people. Why else would he tell me this? He was letting me down gently.

But when I looked up Norm was smiling. "We are planning to turn that space into a group of private offices over the summer. Sarah believes you are the perfect person to help with our pro bono work. You are well-known in Milwaukee and admired in both your public and private life. Your work at Alverno and on community boards has been exemplary. Carol, we would be proud to have you join us at Barkin, Herman, Solochek, and Paulsen."

"Really?" I croaked.

"Yes, really. Welcome aboard."

For the next half hour, we went over specifics. The salary would start at $12,000 a year, with opportunity for advancement and bonuses. It sounded like a fortune to me. As we talked, the tension in my shoulders began to ease. For the first time in months, there was hope. Maybe we were going to make it after all. Yes, Scotty still had cancer, and yes, I had no idea where we would be living next month, but I had a job with the most prestigious PR firm in the state. A huge gamble had paid off. In fact, Norm told me later that my phone call that afternoon was the deciding factor in his decision to hire me. He liked my spunk.

It was close to six when we wrapped up.

"How about a drink to celebrate?"

"A *drink* drink?" I asked, sounding like an idiot.

Norm laughed. "Well, I'm going to have a *drink* drink. You may have whatever you like. We certainly have something to celebrate."

As if by magic, Connie appeared and opened the wall credenza, revealing an array of bottles and glasses. She reappeared with a full ice bucket, leaving the door open on her way out. As people leaned in to say good night to Norm, he introduced me as Barkin Herman's newest account executive.

Norm fixed drinks, and we moved over to the seating area on the other side of the room where we first sat less than a week earlier. Raising his glass, he proposed a toast to the success of my new career.

"I'll drink to that," I said, taking a sip and settling back in my chair.

Could this be real? Me, an account executive, sipping a gin and tonic in a luxurious office on the twentieth floor of the First Wisconsin Center, watching evening fall over Lake Michigan? What were the odds? Why had Heather suddenly agreed to go to McDonald's that Saturday? What made Sarah stop in just then? Why had I told her I needed a job change when it was something I had yet to come to terms with myself? For the second time in as many years, I had landed a job for which I had no training or experience. Hallelujah.

Twenty-six

By the time I pulled into our driveway, it was after seven. The house was dark and quiet. I switched on some lights and sat in the den, bursting with the news of my new job—with no one to tell. Whom could I call? Most of my friends would be having dinner with their families now or out for the evening. Just as I decided to try my mom in Florida, the phone rang. It was Libby.

Libby and I had been friends since the age of ten when we spent summers swimming and playing together at the Fox Point Club. We went through much of grade school and all of high school together, and though we went to different eastern colleges, we drove back and forth from Milwaukee to Boston together in Libby's black Ford convertible. I was a bridesmaid when she married Jimmy, her childhood sweetheart, in October 1959. She would have been my bridesmaid the following June had she not been pregnant with the first of their five children. In 1960, it was considered inappropriate for a pregnant woman to walk down the aisle in a wedding party. Chip and I had vacationed with them often, both as couples and as families. The nine children we had between us were born close enough in age to have fun together. We were Auntie Carolie and Uncle Chipper to their children, and they were Auntie Ibber and Uncle Jimmy to ours. Chip and Jim had known one another since kindergarten, but they were not as close as Libby and I. They were one of the few couples who didn't have to choose sides when we split up. They were and still are the very dearest of friends.

Libby was calling to see how we were doing. When she heard about my new job, she insisted I drop everything and come right over. "We'll celebrate," she said. "Bring the kids."

Who but Libby would invite five extra people to dinner on the spur of the moment? No one I knew. And I knew Jimmy would make us feel like nothing could have made him happier.

"It's just me," I assured her. "The kids are at the lake with Chip. Can I bring something?"

"Just bring you."

As always, walking into their home filled me with warmth—the fire in the fireplace, the sound of happy children, music on the stereo, and beautiful smells from the kitchen. I sank onto the couch and poured out my good news to my friends. For this one night, I could lay down my troubles and feel happy.

As we finished dinner, the doorbell rang. "That must be Bob," Libby said. "He called earlier to talk to Jimmy. We told him to come on over and help celebrate Auntie Carolie's new job. He said he'd had dinner but might drop by later."

Jimmy came back into the room with Bob, a tall, handsome man with silver hair and seriously blue eyes. I had met him several years earlier when his family moved to Milwaukee from Atlanta while Bob was with American Can Company. After a few years, they moved to the company headquarters in Connecticut. I heard he had returned to run Kurth Malting Company in Milwaukee.

Both American Can and the Kurth Malting Company banked at the Marshall and Ilsley Bank, where Jimmy was a rising star. What began as a business relationship for the two men had grown into a genuine friendship. Rumor had it Bob's marriage was in trouble. I knew he was separated but little else about his situation.

The four of us sat in front of the fire, had an after-dinner drink, and chatted about my new job and our mutual acquaintances. The children came in one by one to say their good nights, and still, we nattered on. Later, Libby and Jimmy slipped out to clean the kitchen. Bob and I barely noticed. Each had found a sympathetic ear for the challenges and chaos of our current situations. Finishing the dishes, Jimmy announced they were heading up, but that didn't mean we had to go. We should stay as long as we liked—which turned out to be almost dawn.

And so, born of sadness and need, a friendship was forged that eased our mutual pain and loneliness. Neither could know how important the other would be in our lives.

Twenty-seven

On May 18, 1975, we went to trial. Having completed the requisite marriage counseling and, in my opinion, too few meetings with the guardian ad litem, we fashioned a mutual agreement. Any regrets I may have felt as I rode to the courthouse that day evaporated when Chip and his lawyer arrived with two "minor language changes" to the agreement. Instead of providing child support of $400 per month, Chip would provide $100 per child per month. And instead of splitting the child tax deduction equally on our annual tax returns, my deductions would be for Scotty and Heather, while Chip's would be for Beav and Danny. Were they trying to make money if Scotty died? I was appalled.

"It's a cheap trick," David said. "They're stalling. You don't have to sign this, Carol."

But I didn't have the heart, or the energy, to go back to the bargaining table. More than anything, I wanted the whole thing behind us. Taking a deep breath, I scribbled my initials on the changes and headed for the door.

Libby was waiting in the hall when we came out of the conference room. Just seeing her there made me feel better.

Ironically, Libby was the only one who expressed concern when Chip first proposed. She must have seen warning signs I did not or chose not to see. She knew the insecurities that plagued me back then, my fear of being an old maid. Libby had agreed to serve as a witness on my behalf. Though she understood and supported me in the divorce, it couldn't be easy for her, and I was grateful.

Chip and his lawyer were in the courtroom when we got there. My hands were shaking, and my heart was pounding when the judge entered. David had briefed me on what to expect, but it was all so strange and sterile. The trial part was simple considering the enormity of upheaval our divorce set in motion. Aside from the "minor changes" I had initialed earlier, there were no surprises. Physical custody of the children was awarded to the plaintiff (me), while we would share in major decision-making on their behalf. In addition, they would see their dad on weekends (to be worked out between the two of us), and we would take turns celebrating holidays. In light of Chip's bankruptcy and ignoring the family's reputation and wealth, the court ordered the bare minimum in child support. I did not seek alimony. Whether because I was too proud, too guilty, or just plain naive is hard to say. It was probably a combination of all three.

So there it was. The marriage was over. Almost fifteen years after that beautiful day in June, I was on my own with four children to take care of. How could I ever do that? The kids loved their dad. Pine Lake in the summer and skiing in the winter was the life they knew. That was where they had their friends, their sports, their fun. While I had shared in that life as Chip's wife, let's face it, it was his life. Pine Lake was his heritage. Skiing was his sport. Where was my world? What did I have to offer? Chip hadn't wanted the divorce. Was this really what was best for us? Lying in bed that night, sick with fatigue, I wrestled again with my insecurities. One thing was sure. My focus was on survival now and building a new home warmed by peace, security, and love. It would not be easy.

Twenty-eight

Despite the prospect of a new job, it would be dishonest to pretend life was anything but difficult in those days. Everything was new. I hadn't lived an affluent lifestyle as a child, but there had always been enough. Now I was beginning to understand the beauty and the blessing of that word. Whether it be food, clothes, time, friends, knowledge, support, or patience, having enough is not a given. It is not a right. It is a goal. For the first time, I was making powdered milk and cooking low cost, often meatless, meals, as well as counting pennies. I could see that $400 a month in child support would not go far with four growing children.

Different parts of the day brought different challenges. Get everyone up, fed, and set for the day; be productive and professional at work; get dinner and homework done and cleaned up; and then, only then, could I melt into the sanctuary of my bedroom.

One night, when Scotty came in to kiss me good night, he found me in tears. "Oh, Scotty," I groaned. "How do you cope with life?" Me—asking my fourteen-year-old son with cancer—how to cope with life! I grabbed a tissue and wiped my eyes, trying to get it together.

Scotty sat down beside me, looked me in the eye, and said, "It's easy, Mom. You gotta remember four things." He held up his hand to count on his fingers. "You gotta be tough," he began. "Take one day at a time, never let yesterday screw up today, and never count on tomorrow." With that, he smiled, kissed me, and quietly went back to his room.

I sat there stunned—not only by Scotty's words but by the incredible maturity they reflected. It was the first of many times over the next eighteen months that I was aware of the special gift God gives children suffering from catastrophic illnesses. I was seeing what doctors, nurses, caregivers, and family members have long witnessed as they walk with these children through the ends of their lives—abiding wisdom.

In the morning, Scotty came into my room, threw open my shades, and announced, "The sun is shining, and all you have to do is get through today."

And so I did.

Twenty-nine

With mixed feelings, I said farewell to the wonderful women of Alverno in early June. They had been like family through the most challenging years of my life, but my peers understood my motivation and supported my career move without exception. The fledgling continuing ed department had successfully attracted women to its noncredit programs. To everyone's delight, a number of these women went on to enroll in degree programming. In addition, Alverno's new bachelor of science degree in nursing had brought an influx of three-year RNs seeking to advance their nursing careers. My job had been to sell adult women on Alverno and the benefits of competence-based learning, still a very new concept in higher education. It seemed to be working.

Meanwhile, Norm and I agreed on a start date in early September when my new office would be ready. That gave me two months to adjust to the changes in our lives and find a place to live. The kids spent weekdays in town with me that summer, joining their dad at Pine Lake on weekends. To my surprise, they didn't seem to mind the time in town. We got a permit for Shorewood's public beach, and their friends were delighted to have them in the neighborhood.

Ten days into the break, our house went on the market. Despite Chip's bankruptcy, half of the proceeds from the sale would go to me. The money wouldn't amount to much after the mortgage was satisfied, yet it was what I had. Finding a house in the same school district was a priority. It limited our choices, but the kids had dealt with enough change. At least school and their friends would be familiar.

After touring one small, dark house after another, I couldn't imagine living in any of them, more than once coming home, sitting in my beautiful living room, and crying. Would our children ever forgive me for turning their world upside down?

Then, out of nowhere, a ray of light found its way through the gloom. A friend of a friend of a friend mentioned that a duplex in Shorewood was for sale. I drove by that evening. The house was a red brick colonial with white trim. It looked very much like a single-family dwelling from the street, which made my heart beat a little faster. As it turned out, the realtor (and owner) was Mimi Draper, a woman I had known for years. Though I didn't know her well, I knew her well enough to give her a call at home that night. She agreed to meet me there in the morning.

From the beginning, the house on Newhall Street felt right. The front door opened into a shared vestibule with identical doors leading into the two separate units. As Mimi fussed with the lock, I realized I was holding my breath. *Please, please let it be right.* And then we were standing in a good-sized living room with a wood-burning fireplace and lots of windows. Beyond that were a formal dining room, an eat-in kitchen, and a powder room. Despite the gloom of a rainy morning, the duplex felt bright and open.

Upstairs were three bedrooms and a bathroom with a shower over the tub. The master was large enough for my bed, side tables, and dresser. Danny and Heather would each have their rooms. A sizeable paneled basement could serve as Scotty and Beav's bedroom. Out the back door next to the detached two-car garage, I was astounded to discover a small in-ground swimming pool with a patch of grass.

As if that weren't enough to lift my spirits, a family with two children and a grandmother had been tenants for years and were hoping to stay. With the sale of our house, I could afford the down payment. Rent from the second unit would cover my monthly mortgage payments. It was a little longer walk to Lake Bluff for Danny and Heather, but the Shorewood Middle School and High School were right across the street for Beav and Scotty in the fall.

It seemed too good to be true, and, of course, it was. Mimi needed a clean offer and a quick close. But our house on Prospect had just gone on the market. There was no way to make a down payment and qualify for a loan until it sold. Heaven only knew when that would be. And yet, I knew this was the house for us.

After the showing, we stood on the sidewalk under our umbrellas, talking about mutual friends, the challenges of her real estate career, and the complex pains of divorce. Mimi had bought the duplex after her divorce five years earlier and had lived there ever since. Now there was a new love, and Mimi was living with him. Together, they rented a slip at the Milwaukee Yacht Club and planned to use the money from the duplex to buy a boat. As the rain came down harder, we ran for our cars. "Let's be in touch," I called.

The duplex was on my mind all day. It was perfect for us. That afternoon, we went out to see Mom. She was as excited as I about the possibilities of the duplex and equally disappointed by what seemed like the impossible challenge of making it ours. As generous as Mom had been throughout the divorce, there was no way she could buy the property for us. There must be another way.

And so there was. Mom and I hatched a plan. If Mimi borrowed the money from the bank for the new boat, we might be able to cover her costs and monthly payments until Prospect Avenue sold. Then she could sell the duplex to us and pay off the loan. It was a far-fetched scheme, but somehow, probably because I was so pathetically desperate, Mimi bought into it. Her credit was good, the loan would not be a problem, and she trusted me enough to take the duplex off the market until fall.

Our gamble paid off. In August, shortly after we lowered the asking price a second time, we found buyers for Prospect Avenue. Chip was a realist. He knew there was work to be done on the house and had no interest in paying a handyman to do it—and even less in doing it himself. He had moved from his small apartment in downtown Milwaukee to a larger townhouse in the lake country with room for the kids.

I planned an estate sale for those belongings considered "not necessary for day-to-day living," including some of our wedding gifts. The professionals managing the sale had set restrictions on the number of shoppers allowed in the house at one time. The restrictions were good and bad. It limited chaos inside but left a line of eager buyers waiting in a line that snaked to the corner and beyond. No doubt more than a few were there out of curiosity to see the former Junior League president's household goods. The good Lord blessed the kids and me. We were at school and work on sale day.

One well-meaning, though tactless, acquaintance called to express her sympathies. "I was always envious of you," she said. "You had everything. And now look at you."

Should I laugh or cry? Now, look at me, indeed.

Several years later, Mom told me she had purchased my china and crystal that day and stowed it away. She knew I would disapprove. During that difficult time in my life, material things were just that—material. I focused on being tough, taking one day at a time.

Thirty

By the middle of that summer, another bone marrow biopsy indicated the weekly shots had done little to halt the spread of malignant cells in Scotty's bone marrow. Dr. Fritz began talking about the possibility of sending him to a national cancer center for further diagnosis and treatment. He told us that Sloan Kettering in New York and the National Institutes of Health (NIH) in Bethesda, Maryland, were well-known for cancer research.

In the early 1970s, Congress had authorized significant initiatives to fight cancer and heart disease. As a result, NIH had stepped up cancer research in meaningful ways, including focusing on childhood cancer. Pediatric oncology had a dedicated wing in the Clinical Center. Undoubtedly the best chance for a cure would come from a national cancer center. But we were broke. Even with my new job, it was challenging to cover our costs. What a relief to learn there was no charge at NIH for patients in their research programs. Medical treatment, travel, plus room and board were all covered by government funding. The difficulty would be getting Scotty accepted into a program. Pediatric oncology beds were few and the demands great.

Again we got a break. Dr. Anthony Curreri, president of the Uniformed Services University of Health Sciences in Bethesda, was married to Dad's cousin Dorothy. Tony and his family lived on Lake Mendota in Madison, Wisconsin. Their daughter Cynthia was my age, and I had visited them for a week one summer. The military had called Tony to Bethesda to open the university and get it going. When Mom called, he said he would be returning to Wisconsin at the end of the year but would see what he could do. We knew he was a well-known and highly respected surgeon. In late August, word came that Scotty was accepted in the pediatric oncology Research Program at NIH with a sarcoma of an undiagnosed cell. We never knew for sure what strings Tony pulled but suspected the answer one day when Scotty was a patient in the Clinical Center, and one of the floor nurses told him his "grandfather" was coming for a visit after lunch. When Tony walked in that afternoon, it was the first time he and Scotty had met.

I was ecstatic—a lifeline at last. However, the juggling act that was my life was about to get more complicated. The hard-won date of Scotty's initial appointment at NIH coincided with the opening day of school for Beav, Danny, and Heather and the start of my new career at Barkin, Herman, Solocheck, and Paulsen.

It was not a surprise to learn Chip was too busy to make the trip. It seemed I had reached a mountain too tall. But Mom came to the rescue again, offering to fly from Florida to Milwaukee and then fly with Scotty to Bethesda for his inaugural evaluation. As with so many things in my new world, the solution wasn't ideal. Scotty should have his mom with him for this first visit. But Beav, Danny, and Heather needed me too, and success in my new career was essential if I were to keep us afloat. It was the only option available, and I knew it.

Mom and I stayed in touch by phone while she and Scotty were at NIH and coordinated a treatment schedule. One week a month, for the next three months, Scotty and I would fly to Bethesda and stay at the nearby United Inn while he received outpatient chemo treatments at the Clinical Center.

The actual treatment was painless, requiring only a few hours hooked to an IV drip. The hospital scheduled Scotty's chemo appointments in the early mornings. We were usually back at the motel before noon. Then came the wait. One hour—two, sometimes three hours—would pass before the horrible waves of nausea hit, leaving him hanging over the toilet bowl or lying on the faded floor of the bathroom for the rest of the afternoon and into the night. Though medical research has not yet found a cure for cancer, it has made huge strides in treating the side effects of chemotherapy.

It was such a helpless feeling. Like any mother whose child is suffering, I wanted his horrible nausea to go away or transfer to me. I would wipe his face with a cool washcloth and try to talk him back into bed between bouts. At least the sheets were laundered and looked cleaner than the worn linoleum of the bathroom floor. But he would tell me not to worry, there was nothing I could do, and he would be okay. Finally, I would give up and cover him with the motel blanket. Sometime before morning, he would crawl back into bed and catch a few hours of sleep before beginning the cycle all over again.

Thirty-one

The accommodations weren't elaborate, but no one complained. After all, we were guests of the US government, and for most of us, the financial benefit was huge. The United Inn in Bethesda was devoted almost entirely to outpatients of NIH and their families. A shuttle circled between the hospital and the motel at thirty-minute intervals throughout the day.

We caretakers were moms, by and large. At least in the two-parent families, most dads elected to stay home to earn a living and try to hold things together. An NIH study showed that 85 percent of the parents of catastrophically ill children would divorce. It didn't surprise me. Difficult as it was to travel this road alone, I was grateful to be spared the battles at home, fueled by frayed nerves, money problems, and inadequate communication. Long-distance phone calls were too costly for most. What a comfort it would have been to have cell phones, email, texts, FaceTime, and Skype. We were a disparate group with little in common, save the horror of having kids with cancer.

Before NIH, most of us had simply been going along, leading ordinary little lives with good days and bad, excitement and boredom, satisfactions and disappointments. For some, a bad day meant mud tracked onto the carpet or a fallen cake. For others, it was a visit from a bill collector or an unwanted pregnancy. But none of us, even on our worst days, had imagined a hell like the one we were in, each grappling with a new set of benchmarks to navigate this new world. Was the white count up or down? How about the hemoglobin? Did the IV blow again? What was the sed rate?

It was like arriving in a foreign land with no prior knowledge of the customs or language.

And yet, most mornings, when we gathered in the lobby to wait for the shuttle, we would exchange pleasantries as though getting ready for a field trip to the art museum. "How's it going? Sure needed the rain. Have you tried the cafeteria's meatloaf?"

On occasion, the news would circulate that a child had died. Those were quiet mornings. Our shared pain was less about the lost child than the bewildering reality that death walked so closely among us now—and always the unspoken, guilt-ridden relief that the dead child wasn't ours.

One morning, I woke early, dressed quietly, and took the elevator to the lobby for a cup of coffee and some quiet time with the newspaper. Ian Smith and the battle for apartheid in South Africa were all over the *Washington Post*'s front page, as were stories about the elaborate plans for our country's bicentennial celebration. It was the end of 1975, and Washington DC was busy planning for the country's birthday party. Scotty and I hoped to take in some of the festivities.

Before long, I heard the ding of the elevator and looked up as a woman, wrapped in an old chenille bathrobe, stepped out. Color flooded her cheeks when she spotted me, and she pulled her collar up tightly around her ears like a turtle. "I thought I could get away with no one seeing me this early," she apologized.

"I come down like that lots of mornings," I said. "It's just that today we have an early appointment. I'm Carol; my son Scotty is a patient here."

"I'm Marie," she said. She loosened the grip on her robe, and it settled more comfortably onto her shoulders as she poured a cup of coffee. "My son Wayne just finished his treatment. We're flying home to Nebraska this afternoon." Marie blew on her coffee, took a sip, and perched on the arm of the couch across from me, more comfortable now. "We're going to Mexico next week, Wayne and me," she said. "For Laetrile."

There it was again. Everyone was talking about Laetrile, the wonder drug from Mexico. There was no evidence that the stuff worked, yet this poor woman was flying off to Mexico.

Now Marie seemed to want to talk. Her tale was tragic. She and her husband, Ed, lived in a small town near Omaha. Wayne was their only child, "a little gift from God," born when Marie was forty-two, and they had given up all hope of having a family. A year and a half earlier, the family doctor had discovered a small lump on twelve-year-old Wayne's leg. It was malignant. The doctor advised Marie and Ed to take their son to Omaha for treatment. But they never did. Ed's family, it seemed, didn't put much stock in "fancy" medicine. Ed's sister told Marie about an asparagus diet that cured cancer. She had seen it on TV. So Marie began emulsifying raw asparagus in a blender and feeding it to Wayne.

Then a second lump appeared. This time, they did go to Omaha, and the news was not good. Wayne's cancer had metastasized. The doctors in Omaha referred him to NIH.

"But all the fancy chemo here didn't work neither," said Marie, blinking back tears. The great NIH had not fixed Wayne after all. She was tired and scared. The upcoming trip to Mexico was the family's last hope. They'd mortgaged everything to pay for it. Today we know Laetrile is not a successful cancer treatment.

My heart ached for this poor, uneducated woman. If only they hadn't delayed Wayne's treatment. In my enlightened world, doctors were gods. It never occurred to me to doubt their word or ignore their suggestions. Surely educated people didn't grind asparagus or run off to Mexico. That was voodoo medicine. Or was it? For all my education, was Scotty any better off than Wayne? Did Marie love her son any less than I loved mine? Scotty suffered the ravages of chemotherapy hundreds of miles from everything he held dear because he trusted me, just as Wayne drank asparagus juice and would fly off to Mexico because he trusted Marie. Scotty would face another morning of poison dripping into his veins and another night of vomiting. Did I know if these debilitating treatments would make him well? My legs suddenly felt weak as I started up the stairwell. The fragile thread of control holding me together threatened to give way, casting me adrift in an all-too-familiar sea of loneliness and insecurity. And then I knew. For all my education and connections, there was no difference between Marie and me. There was no right or wrong way. We were both women losing our sons, doing the very best we knew how, and it wasn't enough.

Thirty-two

The alarm went off too early. I swiped at the off button, trying to sink back into my dream—running effortlessly through a field as though there was no end to my energy. My body felt light as a feather. It was a dream I'd had before—one of the few good ones these days. It was hard to let it go. When Scotty groaned and pulled the pillow over his head, I came fully awake. It was January 1976, and we were back in Bethesda.

"I had that cool dream again," I said, throwing off the blanket and turning toward Scotty's bed. "The one where I'm running weightless through a field."

Scotty grunted and turned toward the wall. With my covers off, the room felt cold, the carpet rough under my feet.

"I'm going to hop in the shower. How are you feeling?"

"Tired," he grunted. "Don't doctors ever work in the afternoon?"

"Not around here." I chuckled. "You can come back and sleep this afternoon."

I pulled the plastic rod opening the heavy rubberized shade that covered the large window, hoping the light would get him moving. I needn't have bothered. The eight-story Holiday Inn next door still blocked the sun. In the shadows directly below our window was the United Inn's tiny swimming pool, one of the motel's few amenities. The protective tarp sagged under the weight of wet leaves and garbage. It was hard to be cheerful, so I bent over, kissed Scotty, and headed toward the bathroom.

When I emerged fifteen minutes later, he was hopping on one leg, pulling on his jeans.

"How about breakfast in the new coffee shop?" I suggested. Since fall, construction had been underway, turning the first floor of the annex building into a café for motel guests. It was closer than the Holiday Inn and a much cheerier space, though not attached to the lobby. With its long bar and low lighting, the windowless Holiday Inn dining room was a popular local gathering place at night but seemed more like a cave in the daytime. It always smelled of stale cigarette smoke and whiskey.

Scotty brightened. "Good idea." We took the elevator down and crossed the lobby. Martha called out from behind the front desk.

"How was that freezing-cold Milwaukee, Scotty? Did you have a good Christmas?"

"Yeah, sort of. Did your grandson like the fire truck?"

Martha had enlisted Scotty's help in choosing a Christmas gift for her six-year-old grandson and had gone with his suggestion of a toy fire truck with flashing lights and siren.

"He loves it, but I'm not sure his mom and dad feel the same." Martha laughed.

"They can always hide the batteries," Scotty replied.

That made me smile. Hiding the batteries was a trick we had used on occasion. My aversion to the roars, bangs, and whistles of modern-day toys was legendary in our household. For our boys, if a gift didn't need batteries, it was hardly worth opening. No matter how much we protested, Granny and Grandpa Dick would arrive each Christmas Eve with the latest, noisiest, most costly toys on the market. Increasingly, it seemed, the magic of Christ in Christmas was being buried in the sights and sounds of Madison Avenue.

Not that my childhood had been particularly devout. As children, my sisters and I were dropped off at Plymouth Congregational Church for Sunday school class each week while our parents played badminton with friends at the Normal School gym nearby. It wasn't that Mom didn't think God important in our lives. We said our prayers every night: "Now I lay me down to sleep" and "Our Father who art in heaven, 'hollywood' be thy name." Even now, some seventy years later, if I am exhausted at night, I find myself lacing my fingers together and praying, "God bless Mommy and Daddy and Holly and Lawrie and me."

"See you in a few minutes," I called to Martha, heading for the door. "We're going for breakfast. Hold a seat on the eight o'clock."

"You got it."

Martha was one of many extraordinary United Inn employees we had come to know during our trips back and forth. They seemed to have a genuine interest in the NIH families who stayed there, always ready with a kind word of encouragement or sympathy. We were all so far from home.

Blood tests, scans, and yet another bone marrow biopsy had filled the last three days. The bone marrow biopsy was the most painful of all the tests but still the most important. We had traveled to Bethesda and back three times since fall for weeklong chemo treatments. Today we would find out how effective they had been.

When we arrived at the Clinical Center, we were dumbfounded to learn that Dr. Poplock, Scotty's doctor since coming to NIH last September, was no longer in pediatric oncology. Dr. Peebles was now our doctor. How could someone so interested in Scotty, someone we had come to know and trust, walk away without a goodbye? As we waited for our new doctor, the nurse explained that Dr. Poplock had "rotated out" of pediatric oncology at year-end, and Dr. Peebles had "rotated in." Welcome to the world of the teaching hospital.

Scotty sat on the edge of the examining table, his legs dangling. I took a chair in the corner of the room to wait. Soon Dr. Peebles hurried in and introduced himself, shaking hands with his right hand as he held Scotty's chart open with his left. Then he closed it and looked at Scotty.

"Our cancer team has been examining your case," he began. "We are not satisfied with your progress." This guy got right down to business. I'll say that for him.

"We now know the disease you have is called neuroblastoma, a solid tumor, or sarcoma, usually found in much younger children. The disease rarely presents in teens." His voice was kind, but his words were chilling. It was the first we'd heard the name *neuroblastoma*, though it wasn't until rereading my notes of that appointment years later that I realized we had not had a definitive diagnosis until then.

"We see no purpose in continuing your current chemo regimen. We need to be more aggressive. Today I would like to talk with you and your mom about a new, more aggressive protocol we are testing."

Dr. Peebles was speaking directly to Scotty, which was good. Too often, doctors spoke to me as though he was not in the room, and I knew he resented that. But the words were devastating. We so wanted to hear that the grueling rounds of chemo he had endured had chased the malignant cells from his body. That was not the case. Tears spilled down Scotty's cheeks, his blue-jean-clad legs pumping back and forth over the edge of the table. I stood and took his hand, but he pulled away. He was looking at Dr. Peebles, waiting for him to go on.

"You would be just the third patient, and first young person, to undergo this experimental regimen of chemo. The regimen is so aggressive, it will knock your white count down to zero, leaving you susceptible to any germ you encounter, even those in your mouth. For that reason, we would like to place you in a completely sterile environment called laminar airflow during treatment. You will stay there until your white count returns to a safe level."

Dead silence. I reached again for Scotty's hand, and this time, he held on.

"If people have so many germs in their mouths, why aren't they sick all the time?"

"Good question," Dr. Peebles said. "We all have germs in our mouths. Healthy white blood cells fight those germs every day. When there are no white cells, you need to take pills to fight the germs.

"You are sure to have other questions." He looked my way. "I have some literature for you to look at, both about laminar airflow and about neuroblastoma. Why don't you take it back to the United Inn and talk about it? Write your questions down, and we'll meet tomorrow morning again."

"How about the afternoon?" groaned Scotty.

Dr. Pebbles smiled. "Let's compromise. How about eleven thirty?"

NIH had built the first laminar airflow unit in 1969. Recently, it had been in the spotlight because of a patient named Teddy DeVita, son of the NIH oncologist Vincent DeVita. Teddy had been living in a laminar airflow unit at NIH since 1972. He suffered from acute aplastic anemia, which prevented his body from producing new cells and platelets. The movie *The Boy in the Plastic Bubble*, starring John Travolta, was filmed that year, based loosely on Teddy's life, but not with the blessings of his family. I have never had the heart to see the movie.

Our decision to go ahead with the new treatment might have been different now, but it was 1976, and our choices were limited. There were only a few cancer centers in the country with clinical trials. The National Cancer Institute at NIH was on the cutting edge. We never really considered going home, but there were still questions for Dr. Peebles the next day. He answered them patiently. When we finished, Scotty asked what had happened to the first two patients in the trial. I'd wondered that myself but planned to ask the question when Dr. Peebles and I were alone.

"The first patient didn't make it," Dr. Peebles said. "The second has just begun round two. He appears to be tolerating the treatment. Both are older than you." He made that sound like a good thing, like Scotty's youth would be on his side.

We agreed to go forward with the trial and stayed in Bethesda long enough to schedule the first round. Scotty would not be staying with me at the United Inn anymore. When we came back, he would be admitted to the Clinical Center for a series of preliminary tests and then go into laminar airflow for the five days of chemo and three to four weeks of white cell recovery. I would arrange to be with him for the five days of treatment, but visits during the white cell recovery time would have to be limited to weekends. We faced a whole new set of challenges.

Thirty-three

Some days at NIH were more difficult than others. The day Joe died was one of the hard ones. Joe was probably not his real name because he was from somewhere in the Middle East, but everyone on the floor called him Joe, so we did too. Joe had come to the United States to get an education at American University. He got leukemia instead. After a few years of remission, his cancer had returned with a vengeance, and he had come back to the pediatric oncology floor for treatment.

At nineteen, Joe was old for the unit, but he had begun his treatment there, so there he stayed. He always had a joke or a kind word for the kids, and he often played cards or watched TV with Scotty. It was another of the unlikely alliances forged by people with nothing in common but the cancer cells exploding in their bodies. It had been a really bad week for Joe, and rumor was that NIH was trying to arrange for his mother to come.

The day Joe died, we were watching *The Gong Show* on the little TV hanging over the bed in Scotty's room. When someone closed the door to the hallway, we looked at one another in silence, afraid to say what we were thinking. Door closing was a bad sign on the oncology floor. They closed doors when they wheeled a body to the oversized service elevator at the end of the hall.

My hands moved in quiet rhythm over the rug I was hooking. In-out, in-out, in-out went the latchet hook in mindless repetition. I was making a two-by-four-foot fire engine rug for Danny's room at home. Materials from the occupational therapy department at NIH were made available to family members as well as patients. This perk had proved a godsend. In the early months, I worked on paint-by-number scenes on black velvet. But that kind of detail work now required more patience and concentration than I possessed. The simple task of securing small pieces of yarn to a heavy canvas was about all my weary brain could manage. The rhythm of the stitching was soothing.

Later the nurse told us Joe had died. Scotty turned off the TV and slumped against his pillow. He turned his head toward the wall, hiding the tears I knew were falling. The design on the canvas in my lap blurred—the red yarn of the fire engine suddenly too bright.

Later, we walked to the visitors' lounge at the end of the hall and sat side by side on the couch next to the coffee machine. The smell of coffee, too long on the burner, filled the room. I rose to turn it off. Scotty sat poking at a tear in the plastic couch cover, trying to coax the coarse stuffing back inside. After putting some soap in the scorched carafe, I left it in the sink to soak and sat back down. Scotty turned to me, clear-eyed, and said, "Everyone dies here."

That moment has haunted me many times over the years. At first, it was with a breaking heart for the profound sadness and pain Scotty felt for his friend Joe and the others who had died since he came to NIH. But later—too many years later—my heart understands it was not just the pain and sadness of losing friends that prompted his remark. What he was trying to say was "I'm tired, and I know I am dying."

But I couldn't hear that then. I didn't know how. With all the wisdom of a thirty-eight-year-old mother, it seemed my job to prop him up when he was down, to be his cheerleader. We never talked about dying, Scotty and I. To talk about dying was to surrender, to give up. Mothers were supposed to prepare their children for life, not death.

And so, holding his long, slim fingers in mine, stroking the veins on the back of his hand, bruised by months of IV needles, I said, "Oh no, darling, please don't think that. NIH has the very best doctors—the very best research facilities. Everyone here is working hard to make you better."

It was I, not Scotty, who couldn't talk about his death. That is clear to me now. He knew he was dying, and I robbed him of the chance to speak with me about it. No need to blame me anymore. As the kids say, "It is what it is." But in my bed late at night, when I feel his spirit near, I whisper, "I'm sorry."

Thirty-four

The leaves outside my window at the United Inn were turning red and gold. I bounced harder on the top of my suitcase, trying to get the latches to close. The doctors had liberated Scotty from laminar airflow. His white count, knocked out by his third round of aggressive chemo, had finally fought its way back to a respectable level—enough to let him return to our germ-filled world. We were headed home for a month's break in treatment. We both looked forward to watching his brother Beav play his last football game of the year.

Scotty was ready when I got to the Clinical Center, dressed in well-worn jeans, a T-shirt, and his trademark cowboy boots. A gray suede headband advertising a ski manufacturer held the long brown hair of his wig in place. The length of the hair would have bothered me two years ago, but now it seemed irrelevant. So many things that bothered me two years ago seemed irrelevant now. I held him tight, feeling the bones of his ribs and back. Scotty was proud of his new slim physique. He had been on the chubby side throughout his childhood.

"Looking good," I said, holding him at arm's length, gazing up into his face. He had grown six inches in the last year and a half. How could a body so broken continue to grow like a weed?

At Washington National (now Reagan) Airport, our flight was on time. Scotty grudgingly folded himself into the waiting wheelchair. He needed to conserve energy, and the departure gate was at the far end of the terminal. There would be no way to get him into a wheelchair in Milwaukee. It was okay to be sick at NIH, but he just wanted to be a normal kid at home, and normal kids did not ride in wheelchairs. He was excited to be going home but nervous too. His fifteen-year-old friends were fascinated yet uncomfortable with him these days. While they were fighting to win football games, he was fighting for his life.

Sadly, this trip home, like so many others that year, ended in disappointment. On the day of the football game, Scotty spiked a fever, which meant a trip to the hospital, leaving Beav, who was captain of the eighth-grade team, to play to the cheers of other parents. Chip said he would "try to catch the game," but often, he got waylaid.

The room at Columbia Hospital looked familiar, but we had been in so many, I wasn't sure. The antiseptic smell, which once made me feel faint, was now familiar. His room was on the "teaching floor," which meant interns and residents would be working with him daily, but there would be no charge for his stay. We were without health insurance, and Dr. Fritz understood our financial bind, so he arranged to have Scotty admitted as a teaching patient when he was in Milwaukee. For the past fourteen months, Scotty was at NIH, where there was no charge for research patients. I was learning to accept charity. Pride was a luxury we could no longer afford.

Scotty slumped in a cream-colored vinyl chair in front of the window. I walked over and hugged him. He was burning with fever. We were both quiet—disappointed to miss the game.

"How are we feeling?" chirped a rosy-cheeked aide as she entered the room, a hospital gown, towel, and washcloth in her arms.

"Like hell," Scotty growled, tossing his wig on the bed, leaving his bald head exposed.

This time, I didn't call him on his language or his rudeness. The aide had not checked his chart before entering. Columbia Hospital was one of the best hospitals in southeastern Wisconsin. The rooms were spotless, the halls gleaming, the colors soothing, the equipment cutting edge. Still, I found myself longing for the comfort of NIH. Despite the peeling paint and shabby furniture, the dirty stairwells, and unreliable elevators, everyone at NIH, from cleaning people to surgeons, was graced with uncanny radar that guided them through the minefield of emotions surrounding catastrophic illness.

Thirty-five

Scotty stayed in the hospital that weekend. The doctors monitored his temperature and blood count, keeping in close contact with NIH. On Monday, while I was in my office dictating to my secretary, Cecelia, Dr. Peebles called from NIH. "Scott's sed rate continues to drop," he said. "He is not getting enough oxygen in his blood."

Blood counts, sed rates, platelet counts—parents of cancer kids get a crash course in hematology whether they want it or not. Dr. Peebles was kind but firm when he told me Scotty needed to get back to Bethesda right away.

Hanging up, I burst into tears. We had planned a whole month at home, enough time to get caught up with my work and justify the firm's faith in my ability to drop in and out and still make a contribution. Ben should have fired me long since, but that wasn't Ben. He was a brilliant PR man, but he cared more about people than the bottom line for all his flamboyance and drive. They hired me from Alverno, knowing my son was battling cancer, and had been nothing but supportive.

Cecelia set down her dictation pad. She had been in this with me for the last year and understood better than anyone the difficult tightrope I walked. She came around the desk and laid her hand on my shoulder. The kindness of her touch melted whatever strength was left. "I have no sitters, no money, and piles of work."

"It'll get done, Carol. You take care of getting a sitter, and I'll handle the airlines. Will he need oxygen?"

"Yes," I called to her back as she hurried out.

Where had she come from, this angel of mercy with her tight sweaters, too-short skirts, and butterfly tattoo? She could switch gears as fast as she could type. Her heart was pure gold. Arranging for oxygen on an airline flight was no small task, but if anyone could figure it out, it was Cecelia.

I felt numb and filled with the nagging fear of inadequacy that followed me everywhere these days. The bank of lights blinking along the bottom of my phone attested that it was Monday morning, and soon the holidays would be upon us. My clients would be gearing up for new campaigns without the benefit of my creative ideas. The kids were preparing for their Christmas pageants and band concerts without my support. The buzz of the interoffice line startled me. I had been staring into space for thirty minutes while Cecelia had made reservations for one o'clock the following afternoon. The oxygen would be waiting on board.

Getting reliable sitters on short notice was a nightmare. Chip and his new wife, Patty, couldn't take the kids until the weekend, and it was only Monday. I started through my phone book but no luck. Once again, the kids would have to split up, staying with a different friend. It wasn't ideal, but they would be well cared for and safe even if not together.

The rest of the afternoon flew by as I arranged with colleagues to cover my accounts. For most, that meant picking up where they had left off less than a week ago. No one ever complained, and there was no time to worry about the burden my schedule placed on these kind people. God bless them all.

The next day, an ambulance took us to the airport from the hospital. Scotty asked if they would blow the siren, and he smiled when they did but didn't ask again. I sat holding his hand and watching the curious faces of people on the street. His high-top tennis shoes stuck off the end of the stretcher, dirty and worn. He'd be upset I left his cowboy boots at home. To this day, when an ambulance passes, I pray for the frightened people inside.

The driver drove the ambulance out onto the tarmac. By the time the passengers boarded, Scotty and I were in our seats with his oxygen tank strapped into the empty seat between us. His seat back reclined all the way. The seat behind us was left empty.

Scotty slept most of the way to Washington—or pretended to. His eyes stayed closed until the plane touched the tarmac. He had no desire to talk and hated the curious stares of others. The flight attendants requested we stay seated while the aisle cleared to make room for the nursing attendants from NIH. For the first time since Friday, Scotty broke into a grin as he recognized the two men boarding the plane with a rolling stretcher, NIH stitched on the pockets of their jackets.

"Hey, man. I guess you missed us so much you couldn't stay away," said the first man, punching Scotty softly on the arm.

"No one could miss your ugly puss," Scotty retorted, obviously happy to see familiar faces.

Big as they were, these men handled Scotty with exquisite care as they eased him onto the stretcher and switched his oxygen to their portable supply. "Let's get you home," the bigger man said. "Doc Peebles is callin' for you." He turned to me. "How you doin', Ms. Swallow?"

"I'm doing fine," I said, reaching for my coat in the overhead compartment. "Let's get you home," he had said. Was this home now? In many ways, NIH had been our home this past year. Here the burdens, the fears, the responsibilities, and the uncertainties of Scotty's cancer seemed less onerous because they were shared with others whose lives were dedicated to lightening our load.

Grabbing our things, I hurried to catch up with the trio as they headed for the Jetway; two strapping young men were bantering with a fifteen-year-old boy, sick and scared, juggling the demons of adolescence and mortality with the body of a man and the mind of a boy.

Thirty-six

X-rays, CT scans, more blood work, and another painful bone marrow biopsy filled the first week back. This time, there was an urgency that had not been there before. At the end of the week, Dr. Peebles called us into his office.

"Thank you for coming," he said, fussing with some papers on his cluttered desk. The tiny room felt airless with no windows and a bluish glow from the neon lights overhead. I thought of Dick Fritz's office back home with its large windows and green plants. Dr. Peebles waited for us to get settled.

"The chemo has done its job," he said. "Scotty's bone marrow biopsy shows no sign of cancer cells."

This was good news. Great news. Why did Dr. Peebles look so somber? Shifting in his desk chair, he looked at Scotty.

"The strong medicine we used in your treatment has weakened your immune system. We believe you may have contracted a rare disease called pneumocystis pneumonia. It is a fungus that people with weakened immune systems seem less able to fight. It's a different kind of pneumonia, one that prevents oxygen from getting into your bloodstream."

Scotty was immensely proud to have been the first patient to make it through all three courses of the experimental treatment. His last bone marrow biopsy was free of cancer cells. Wasn't that precisely what we had hoped and prayed for? Now they were telling us there was a price to pay? Dr. Peebles was saying that the chemical assault had so compromised the immune system that he had developed this strange kind of pneumonia, which, though rare in 1976, would soon become tragically familiar as a major killer of those fighting HIV/AIDS.

Why had no one told us about pneumocystis pneumonia? After fighting so valiantly for months, surviving three debilitating courses of chemo, withstanding endless weeks in the total isolation of laminar airflow, now oxygen isn't getting into his blood? I wanted to scream or kick something, but Scotty sat utterly still, looking at Dr. Peebles, waiting for him to go on.

"We have seen this in other chemo patients," Dr. Peebles continued, "A serum has been developed in England, which has proven successful in some cases. We want to try it. However, we will need permission for a lung biopsy to verify the diagnosis."

There it was again, a thread of hope. The agony of another painful decision. When was it enough? My experience with medical research had been nonexistent fourteen months ago. The NIH research program had seemed so hopeful—our only chance. It was a beacon of light in the darkness. I asked at the time how it worked. Did some patients get real medicine and others placebos? If that were the case, we wouldn't consider it. But the doctors insisted that would not happen. They would not compromise Scotty's chances to fight his cancer in any way. I trusted them; we both did. But now, each day, the fight seemed harder. We had won a few battles, but we were losing the war.

Scotty looked at me but spoke to Dr. Peebles. "Let's do it," he said.

"You don't have to do this, Scotty," I began, hoping to buy some time to think about it, to talk about it, trying one more time to put off the inevitable.

"Yes, I do, Mom." His voice didn't waver. There were no tears in his eyes this time. He reached out and took my hand in his, and I knew this wasn't the frightened little boy who came to NIH fourteen months ago. This was a young man facing what no fifteen-year-old should ever have to face with more courage and grace than others twice his age. We scheduled the lung biopsy for early the following Monday. Should it confirm the diagnosis, they would order the medicine from England. One thing was sure: Scotty would not be back in Milwaukee for Thanksgiving, which was the following Thursday, and perhaps not even for Christmas. I spent the weekend laying a backup plan.

My first call was to Chip, both to fill him in on the new diagnosis and ask if he could come and stay with Scotty the week after Thanksgiving. He had made just one visit to NIH early in the laminar airflow treatments. He flew out with his mother for a weekend.

Chip chose that weekend to tell his mother he planned to marry Patty, a widow with three boys who skied on the same racing circuit with our boys. Janet was not pleased.

When the kids began to mention Dad's new friend Patty with increased frequency, I could not help asking about her. "She's nice," they chorused. "She wears leather pants and size-four cowboy boots!" I hated her instantly—although, when we met, Patty did seem nice. She was a small, pretty woman with long black hair—the exact opposite of me in every way.

From the beginning, Patty's feisty Irish temper was on a collision course with Janet Swallow. After a few early run-ins, Patty announced she would no longer put up with Janet's rages. If Chip wanted to spend time with his mother, he would have to do it alone. As far as I know, she stuck to that.

As always, Chip was busy with work and the opening of ski racing season, but he agreed to come the week after Thanksgiving. Meanwhile, Bob made arrangements to come to Bethesda for Thanksgiving and fly home with me. He and I had been seeing one another regularly since the night at Jimmy and Libby's, and he was my rock. As always, my mom was there for me. She would follow Chip's visit and stay through Christmas. Then I would return until he could come home.

The biopsy confirmed the diagnosis, and the doctor ordered the medicine from a lab in England. The lung surgery took longer than expected, leaving an arcing scar from Scotty's front to his back. When it was over, he was exhausted. What little energy he had left was gone.

Bob arrived Wednesday, and we spent Thanksgiving weekend sitting with Scotty as he slept and watched TV. Talking was an effort, as he was on oxygen full-time now. Every few hours, Bob would take me for a walk or to the cafeteria. Tired down to my bones, I seemed incapable of moving on my own. When we flew out on Saturday, it was with the confidence that Chip would be arriving Monday or Tuesday.

Thirty-seven

But Chip didn't get there Tuesday. Or Wednesday. Or Thursday. It was hard for Scotty to talk through the oxygen mask, much less talk on the phone, so much of our communication that week was with the nursing station. They said Chip was "held up on business." They also reported that Scotty now had a roommate—fourteen-year-old Jack from Fort Lauderdale, Florida. Jack had been Scotty's very first roommate when they both were new at NIH. Jack had leukemia. As often as the two were at NIH since then, it was the first their paths had crossed. They had formed a friendship then, and sick as they were, the boys seemed pleased to see one another again. For me, there was comfort in knowing Scotty wasn't lying there all alone. So far, the serum from England had not succeeded in improving his oxygen levels. Everyone was worried.

When Chip finally got there, it was Saturday. Patty called to tell me he was there and that Scotty appeared to be okay. How unfair it was of me to frighten Chip by exaggerating the seriousness of Scotty's condition. I was speechless. If only that were true. By Sunday afternoon, Chip called to tell me to come back. Scotty's condition was worse.

Fortunately, there was an empty seat on a flight Monday morning, and the kids could return to the homes of our friends they had just left. My friend Susy drove me to the airport. Despite all the years of friendship and memories we shared, there was little we could say on that drive. She knew what lay ahead for me, and I felt her love.

Chip was in Scotty's room talking with Jack's mother, Mary, when I got to the hospital. Scotty gave me a smile and a hug but had little energy for conversation. Jack was sleeping. Like Scotty, he had lost a great deal of weight and was very pale. He was getting pain medication through an IV drip. When the nurse came in, Chip asked if we could see Dr. Peebles in his office.

"Good idea," I said. "Maybe he can explain what we do if the serum doesn't begin to work."

But when we settled into the small office, Chip announced he had some pressing business at home. Did Dr. Peebles think it would be okay if he went back to Milwaukee that night and returned Wednesday? I was stunned.

Dr. Peebles looked at Chip.

"Your son is gravely ill, Mr. Swallow. I cannot possibly tell you that will be okay. The decision must be up to you."

"Then I'll be back by noon Wednesday," Chip said. That was it. He got up, shook the doctor's hand, and left the office. I followed him into the hall.

"Could I have some time alone with Scotty?" he asked.

"Of course. Come get me in the lounge when you are ready to leave."

Thirty minutes later, Chip came to say goodbye. "Hold the fort," he said. "I'll be back Wednesday morning." I headed back to the lounge to call the United Inn.

"We have no rooms available tonight," said the desk clerk, sounding harassed.

"But my son's father, Kingston Swallow, is just checking out. Could I have his room?"

"He checked out this morning. We have no rooms available tonight."

From my first visit to NIH, I had never stayed anywhere but the United Inn. "Maybe they have room at the Holiday Inn," I tried.

"They're full too," the woman said. "These weeks between Thanksgiving and Christmas are always crazy."

Just then, Mary walked into the lounge and poured a cup of coffee. I hung up and went to sit with her. Jack did not have much longer, she said. They had rented a house in Bethesda and planned to stay there for the remainder of his illness. Her husband had moved in today.

"Jack will never come home again," she said, "so we will bring home to him."

When Mary heard about my problem finding a room, she brightened. "I didn't check out of the United Inn yet. I packed but never checked out. Take my key for as long as you need. We can settle up later."

"That would be wonderful, Mary." The United and Holiday Inns were the only places to stay in the area, but only the United Inn ran a shuttle to and from the Clinical Center. We hugged and headed back to sit with our sons. Once again, an angel had landed on my shoulder. I had a room at the inn.

Later the smell of popcorn filled the air. It was coming from the nurses' lounge. "That smells good," Scotty said. "Can I have some?" They told me he hadn't eaten much all week, and tonight he had turned away his favorite grilled cheese and tomato soup. When I kissed him good night and headed for the United Inn, he had pulled down his oxygen mask and was happily munching on a bowl of popcorn. It was the happiest he had been in weeks.

"See you in the morning, sweetheart. I love you."

"I love you too, Mom."

Thirty-eight

But Scotty died in the morning.

After I'd said my final goodbye to the cold, still body that had held my beautiful boy, Dr. Peebles walked me back to the nurses' lounge and sat beside me on the soft fabric couch. We did not talk, but his familiar presence was comforting. At some point, his beeper went off, and he excused himself. One of the nurses, again one I didn't know, came in to see if she could do anything for me. She explained that the visitors' lounge at the end of the hall was getting a new floor. It would be closed all day. "You're welcome to stay here as long as you like," she offered, laying a hand on my shoulder.

The visitors' lounge at the end of the unit wasn't fancy, but it was welcoming, filled with large windows and an eclectic mix of chairs and couches that people could move to accommodate both large and intimate groupings. There were magazines and jigsaw puzzles, coffee, tea, and soft drinks. It offered a much-needed break-space for families and patients alike. It was where patients and families formed friendships and found many a sympathetic ear. I listened to and comforted many over the months we were there. But now it was my turn, my loss, my child—and the lounge was closed for the day. Where was everyone?

A black phone sat on the desk across from the couch in the nurses' lounge, lit up by a row of blinking lights. It reminded me of my office. The nurse showed me which button to push for an outside line and encouraged me to call family members and friends. I must have called Patty, but I don't remember the call. We somehow arranged for her to contact Chip to pick up the children at school and take them back to their house. It seems Chip was already on a flight to NIH, but the airline could get him off when the plane stopped in Detroit and fly him back to Milwaukee. It was Chip who would tell Beav, Danny, and Heather that their brother died. I can only imagine how painful that was. We all lived with the hope Scotty would get better and come home again. None of us prepared for the emotional devastation of his death.

At a break during an early morning business meeting in Chicago, Bob called the nursing station. They forwarded the call to me in the lounge. "He is gone," I said—no need for an explanation. We had talked for an hour the night before. Without hesitation, Bob told me he would come.

"I'll be there as soon as I can. Why don't you go back to the United Inn and wait for me?"

The idea was unthinkable. Walk away and leave Scotty there? "No. No. I'll be here. I'm in the nurses' lounge."

There were other calls to make. Details of the conversation with my mom escape me, though she did say she was coming. I also called Father Murray Trelease, rector of Saint Paul's Episcopal Church in Milwaukee. We scheduled the funeral for the coming Saturday morning and arranged for him to stop over to see the kids and me on Thursday night.

Murray had been a tremendous comfort to us over the months of Scotty's illness. He spent time with Scotty when he was at the hospital in Milwaukee and corresponded with him at NIH. They were friends. When I expressed concerns about Scotty not being baptized, Murray assured me that he was in God's eyes. I knew they had talked about God and baptism. His assurances were comforting. Surely a loving God would not punish an innocent child for something his parents did or didn't do. But then, how could a loving God let a child suffer the way Scotty did?

Someone must have brought me something to eat along the way, but what and when are a mystery. I couldn't think beyond that room, couldn't grasp that Scotty was gone. The sensation was strong that time stood still. At some point, my legs needed stretching, and I stepped into the hall. Mary came out of a door down the corridor, hugged me, and told me how sorry she was. Just then, the double doors at the end of the hall swung open, and in walked Bob.

"What took you so long?" I said, running to him and clinging to his coat, still cold and damp with rain. He smiled. It had been less than three hours since he called from Chicago. Miraculously he packed his bag, checked out of his hotel, got to O'Hare, bought a ticket, and ran the length of the concourse while they held a flight for him. When he landed at National, he still needed to find a cab and make his way to Bethesda in the pouring rain. For the first time, in a day so filled with unfamiliar faces, the warmth of his arms and the shared sadness in his beautiful blue eyes cracked the shell I was suspended in, and finally, I cried.

We went back into the nurses' lounge. When the nurse came in, I introduced Bob and asked if he could see Scotty. For some reason, it didn't occur to me that Scotty wasn't still lying cold and still on the bed behind the closed door across the hall. It was devastating to learn they had taken him away. Just hours earlier, I was stroking his hand and crooning, "It's all right. Momma's here."

Now—after months and months of fighting this fight with him, and for him, in every imaginable way—I didn't even know where he was. The pediatric oncology wing bustled with its usual activity and purpose all around us, but my time there was over.

Bob helped me sign the necessary papers, and someone brought a paper bag with Scotty's things. His old tennis shoes, silver ID bracelet, and blue plastic name tag, with "SCOTT SWALLOW SUPERSTAR" etched in white letters that he wore when he was upstairs helping in the children's ward, were all there was. It seemed such a little bag, but I clung to it as Bob led me past the newly tiled visitors' lounge, down the elevator, and out into the cold rain.

Thirty-nine

By morning, the sky was clear, the rain replaced by cold sunshine, as though there had been enough tears. But I knew there would never be enough tears. As the plane circled Washington and headed toward Wisconsin, the same sensation washed over me as the day before when we left the hospital. It was as though I was deserting Scotty—leaving him behind. As a research patient, NIH would do a thorough autopsy on Scotty before cremating him and sending his ashes to Forest Home Cemetery in Milwaukee for burial. I knew all that. But my head and my heart were not in sync. I doubt the trip home would have been possible without Bob's capable and loving care. The strength that had sustained me over the last two years, the strength that always seemed able to be replenished, was slipping away. It was distressing to watch people bustling through the airport, as though it was just another day. It wasn't just another day. It was the first day without Scotty.

Bob dropped me off at my house.

"Should I stay?" he asked, before heading back to his office.

"I'll be fine. You have done too much already. Thank you for bringing me home."

"If you need anything at all, give me a call. I'll stop in later." With that, he hugged me and was gone.

The silence in the house was deafening. Things looked just as they had when I left Monday morning but felt different—very different. Suddenly, the numb feeling, the sensation of being suspended in time, gave way to an unimaginable sense of loss that took my breath away. I sank onto the sofa, my head in my hands, and the tears flowed unchecked.

Whether it was ten minutes or an hour later, the doorbell rang. It was Chip. As our eyes met, I saw the raw pain on his face and knew he was the only person who could fully understand what I was feeling because he was feeling it too. He opened his arms, and I stepped into them. We didn't speak. All the anger and bitterness of the last two years dropped away as we held each other, sharing the one emotion we had left to share: the agony of losing our son. I will always remember the kindness and honesty of that warm embrace. Whatever was behind or lay ahead for each of us, what had been was good and brought us four beautiful children. Our mutual love of them was a tie that would never be broken.

Forty

My memories of the days leading up to the memorial service are a blur. Instead of flying to Bethesda to spend Christmas with Scotty, Mom flew to Milwaukee for his funeral. Father Murray spent an evening with us, talking with the children and going over plans for the service. As ill-prepared as I was for Scotty's death, I was less prepared for his funeral. Murray helped us choose the readings and hymns. It was hard to put one foot in front of the other. The service was a memorial rather than a funeral service because there was no body to lay to rest. We selected an eight-by-ten photo of Scotty in his wig and headband to place next to the altar. While each of the children did, and would, process their brother's death differently, we were all sharing in the shock of the sudden loss.

Libby called to tell me she and Jimmy were inviting everyone back to their house for a luncheon after the service. "It's the perfect spot," she insisted. "You and Chip are both comfortable here, and so are your kids. We have plenty of room."

"But—"

"No argument from you, young lady. Murray will print the invitation on the bottom of the service pamphlets."

As much as I wanted to argue with Libby, how could I? We did not have the space, the energy, or the wherewithal to host a gathering after the service, and Chip and Patty lived a thirty-minute drive from Saint Paul's. With a grateful heart, I found myself accepting yet again the seemingly endless kindnesses of others.

Forty-one

The day of the service dawned cold and dry. Mom and I got the kids, and ourselves dressed and at Saint Paul's by ten. The family was to gather in the church library before the eleven o'clock service. I asked Bob to be there too. Difficult as the next few hours would be, they would be easier with him by my side. Soon Chip and Patty arrived, followed by his sister, Susy, and her children. Mother Swallow came next with her half-sister Lyle and her family. I hadn't seen Janet since the divorce and was surprised and grateful for her warm embrace and kind words. Animosity had no place in our hearts. It was a day of honoring and remembering a young man dear to us all.

Shortly before eleven, we entered the church, filing into the front pews reserved for family. Bob and I, Beav, Dann, and Heather and then Chip and Patty. The organ was playing, and the large church was overflowing with friends and acquaintances, many with children in tow. It wasn't long before the organ finished and the service began. After the readings, Father Murray stepped to the podium to offer a homily. I could hear people coughing and shifting in their pews, pulling out the coloring books and crayons, imploring their kids to be quiet. Did people wonder, as I did, what on earth this man could say that would lessen the tragedy of Scotty's death? Could he justify a God who let this happen to a child?

Father Murray stood quietly for a moment, raised his arms as though to embrace the congregation, and began:

It was a glorious fight, And it would appear everyone lost. Certainly the feeling of loss and grief is deep and painful. So perhaps you will think I am out of my mind when I say it was a victory, and we are here, not to mourn, but to praise God for our victory.

I believe in life after death with God. All three of our lessons speak of it. But I'm not thinking primarily of life after death, but of the victory Scotty and his family won through God's love and grace during these past two years.

The victory was, very simply, to live humanly to the end of his life. Scotty maintained his humanity though faced with every possible threat: a pernicious and deadly disease, fear, pain, isolation from those he loved, discouragement, and long periods of weakness and disability. All of the destructive forces which can take the heart right out of a person, Scotty faced and did not give in. He had a lot of help. His mother and father, his sister and brothers, doctors, nurses, and many friends were all ministers of God's great love and all share in the victory as you all share in the grief.

A great deal of wisdom was given and received during the fight. Even before he became ill, Scotty said, "You have to be tough. You can't let yesterday mess up today. Take one day at a time." He and his family learned to love each other as they were, day by day. So many of us see our children or our parents as future potentials or past reflections, looking at what they were or what they may become, or ought to become, or we want them to become. But because time and future were so uncertain, Scotty and his family had to know each other, and love each other, as they were each day. And that is very wise.

Can any of us be so certain of tomorrow that we dare risk not loving and not living today?

Perhaps the greatest sense of victory was seen in Scotty's peacefulness at the end. It is a bitter thing to lose a game or a battle. But if you have fought to the end, given everything you have, lived each day as completely as you can, you are at peace. You were truly alive and there is nothing to blame yourself for, even if you lose. That is the victory of being human right up to the gates of death.

The lessons we will hear do not hold out false hope, suggesting that God will remove danger, disease, and death from those who have a little more faith. They are testimonies to the great creator God who loves us so much he comes down into the midst of our battle and sorrows and suffers with us.

The symbol of his great suffering love is the cross of Christ. He gives us victory in the midst of, and in spite of, our great tragedies and finally claims us as his own, beyond the limits of this life.

Father Murray's words of wisdom lifted the sense of darkness hanging over Saint Paul's that cold December morning, offering comfort at a time when none seemed possible. Later, Bob had those words matted and framed for me along with an artist's sketch of Scotty. It still hangs in my home.

As time passes and I say goodbye to old friends and loved ones with greater frequency, I grasp the meaning of Father Murray's homily more deeply. "Being human right up to the gates of death" is not a blessing shared by all.

Forty-two

When Libby and Jimmy offered to host a gathering after the service, I doubt any of us predicted the size of the crowd that appeared. We were astonished by the number of young people. Classmates, who hadn't known what to say to Scotty over the last two years, turned out in force to bid him farewell. They clustered in a small den off the family room, whispering among themselves. For most, it was the first time they had attended the funeral of a peer.

It was with great sadness the kids and I realized later that Jerry Sawalish, the one classmate who had stuck with Scotty throughout his illness, wasn't there. It was Jerry who wrote to him at NIH, spent hours on long-distance calls into the night, and waited on our doorstep each time Scotty returned home. Jerry didn't hang out with the in-crowd, and though his mother had come with him to the church service, she must have returned to work, leaving him without a ride to the luncheon. It is something I will always regret. Scotty would have wanted Jerry there.

Valued coworkers from Alverno and Barkin Herman came, showing their friendship and offering their support. To my surprise, Ben Barkin came with Norm. As they were leaving, I thanked them profusely for the understanding and generosity they had shown me over the past year. The firm had continued to pay me a full-time salary for what was not full-time work. Ben smiled and, opening his big arms, pulled me into a bear hug.

"You've been through a lot, kid," he said. "I want you to take the rest of the year off. Spend time with your family. Then," he continued with a chuckle, "I want you back in the office where we plan to work your butt off."

I laughed. "You got it!"

Today the hug would have constituted sexual harassment, the term "kid" considered disrespectful, and the reference to my butt entirely out of line. But in 1976, I welcomed the hug, understood the language, and found the promise of a job more than comforting.

In bed that night, with Mom asleep by my side, I thought about Father Murray's comforting words and thanked God for getting me through the day—for Libby and Jimmy's overwhelming friendship and kindness, for Bob's unwavering strength and support. I prayed for solace as Beav, Danny, and Heather, my beautiful, healthy children, found their way through their grief.

Looking Back

May 2021

Those years drew a line through my soul, redefining forever who I was and who I would become. No longer was I the insecure, broken wife who set out to find a job, nor the overwhelmed and helpless mother fighting an impossible battle along with her son. I was a strong, capable woman with a successful career. I had learned humility by accepting charity from others and trust through opening my life to strangers. Perhaps most important, I had learned the profound joy of living and loving day by day.

Since then, I have spoken with many parents who have lost children—some suddenly, others through a prolonged illness. Almost without exception, these parents can look back and follow a thread of hope or happiness born from the devastation of their loss.

When I began to write my story, it was the unexpected support, the fortuitous timing of events, the mysterious twists and turns that I remembered—the many people who entered my life at just the right moment, the many circumstances that shifted mysteriously for the better. The days when things were at their darkest, and a ray of sunshine would find its way through the clouds. It was those little miracles, woven seamlessly into my life, that preserved my sanity and provided me the strength to face unimaginable truths. Viewed through the kinder, gentler lens of age, it was all the little miracles that turned my path of hardship and loss into one of survival, hope, and victory. For that, I am eternally grateful.

CPSIA information can be obtained
at www.ICGtesting.com
Printed in the USA
LVHW091818080222
710588LV00003B/341